How the TRUTH Will Set You & Your Career Free

Career Success and Job Search
Sanity Secrets for the Critical Few
(You Know Who You Are...)

BARRY C. KLEIMAN

TESTIMONIALS
(What they are saying...) about

Barry Kleiman

"I've known Barry for many years. His coaching in my life has had profound effects and I can honestly say that I owe a great deal of my current business success to his involvement. Aligning with Barry Kleiman is a recommendation I can make wholeheartedly."

Donna Orender - Founder Generation "W" Former President - WNBA (Women's National Basketball Association) 2005 - 2010

Like the many people who have been helped by Barry, I feel fortunate to know him and recommend his services without reservations.

Robert D. Haas - Chairman of the Board, Emeritus - Levi Strauss & Co.

"Barry is supportive, professional, engaging, inspiring, dedicated, fearless, insightful and relentless in providing unique strategies to help you achieve your career objectives. He has been the "tipping point" in helping me to define, achieve and navigate the "MORE" that I want in my career. I am thankful to Barry for helping me continue to thrive as I transform in my career!

Barry is passionate about helping others reach their career & life goals. Because he is passionate about his life mission, he has established an exclusive business model that allows him to have a special one-on-one relationship with all of his clients.

Barry is not a hired gun, he is a partner, friend and coach committed to helping you reach your dreams and making the changes that you want to make."

Raquel Daniels - Marketing & Customer Strategist | Storyteller | Multicultural Marketer | Integrator | Marathon Runner

"Passion, honesty, education, and respect are qualities that Barry brings to his coaching, his career and his personal life. If you are looking to change directions or feel there is something better out there for you, contacting Barry is the first place I would start.

Shaw Kobre - Director of Marketing
Charter & Company

"Barry Kleiman is an incredible person, nothing less. I believe he has the know how to take on any problem and solve it. He has a very special gift to motivate people around him and his work is a demonstration of his intelligence, compassion, and love to help others succeed. He is one of the most positive people I know and positive spreads positive... Thank you for all the great suggestions and assistance."

Heidi Merriman - Quality Control, Guest Relations,
Accounting and Human Resources Professional

"I have known Barry for a number of years and have worked with him on numerous projects from recruiting to professional development. In the end, there is no one I trust more than Barry in these two fields. Barry is very insightful and has regularly added value to my organizations. I highly recommend Barry for your professional development and professional recruiting needs."

Ron LaVelle Partner,
Family Office Practice at Seiler LLP

"I've had the sincere pleasure of knowing Barry for almost 20 years and have always been impressed by his integrity, wisdom and real gift for connecting with people. He's given me sage advice that has helped me both personally

and professionally. He also single-handedly fixed my backhand in a matter of minutes. Barry just has a knack for honing in on the root cause of an issue and offering up solid resolutions that work."

Michele Drohan - Senior Partner Manager, Sling TV

"Barry is amazing on so many different levels! He motivates others to aim for their dreams by providing the right framework and steps to realistically get there. As a mentor and career coach, he truly listens, spends a lot of time asking the right questions, and tries to find careers that match what truly is in the best interests of his clients. He has an incredible heart and passion for mentoring young adults especially in his work with AmeriCorps. He is a great tennis player and student of many sports who applies lessons learned there to life in general and to career planning. For someone who is so gifted in so many areas, he is so humble and approachable. I am so fortunate to know Barry and have worked with him"

Michael Wong - Associate Director,
UNC Kenan-Flager MBA Career Management Center

Barry's extensive knowledge in the areas of professional coaching enables him to be highly effective in facilitating change and improvement for individuals as well as organizations. . I've found Barry to be easy to work with, and his engaging teaching style is results driven. His integrity is of the highest order and one of his finest qualities.

Kevin Lee - CEO Stat Revenue

"Through our many conversations, Barry has proven to be a very honest, motivational, and knowledgeable advisor to work with. He is able to draw on his own experiences, both good and bad, as well as those of others to help you *really think about what is important to you when it comes to your career and personal life. Very many people will unintentionally make career choices that are not ideal for them, primarily because they do not realize the importance of making a long term plan that considers all aspects of your life. Ultimately, everyone is responsible for the choices he or she makes, but with Barry's guidance you will be in a much better position to make the choices that are right for you"*

Glenn E. Hafstad - Director, Financial Planning & Analysis

It was my good fortune to be recommended to Barry in 1998 when I was making the transition from public accounting to the corporate accounting world. During a time of dramatic change and "irrational exuberance", Barry was a voice of wisdom and calm. He helped me understand what was most important to me - both personally and professionally, and has continued in that regard ever since. As a result of working with Barry, I found my career passion, realized the power of following your own personal calling, and came to understand the great joy of simply surrounding yourself with good people who share your passion for whatever undertaking you may be following. Barry is first and foremost a tremendous person, who has great perspective about life and a passion for living it. I assure you that getting to know Barry, in whatever capacity that might be - coach, mentor, friend, client - will enrich your life in many, many ways.

Mike Byron - Chief Accounting Officer

"I have known Barry for almost 30 years but it wasn't until my 20th year of knowing Barry that we clicked and he found me an excellent position with a medical device company. However, it wasn't the job find that I attribute to Barry but the counseling, honesty, decency, trustworthiness and most importantly, life-long friendship that I will always cherish most about Barry. If you would like to do business with Barry immediately or sometime in the future you will get more advice, inspiration, insight, dedication and overall professional demeanor than you could ever hope to imagine. I say this honestly and without hesitation, that I consider Barry one of my best contacts on LinkedIn"

Joe Drinkwater - Field Associate

"I have relied on Barry's advice as a business coach and mentor for many years. Barry knows how to discover what is Unique about each person and how to help them Capitalize on that strength. Barry is optimistic, but also practical and realistic about helping you clarify your goals and objectives. Most importantly, Barry will help to keep you preoccupied and focused on a better future. I trust Barry because of his Integrity (He tells the truth and keep his word) his maturity (He respects the emotions of others) and his ability to energize people. Anyone will benefit from knowing and working with Barry"

Dana Shertz - COO/Sales Strategist

"Yes, Barry is great, but equally important is that you will enjoy working with him. Very quickly, Barry ends up knowing who you are and is generous enough to share his tremendous insight about what you bring to the party as well as opportunity options. Most value add recruiter, ever. Emotionally intelligent and a wonderful human being."

Teresa Conville - Finance Manager

"I worked with Barry when he offered his services for free for the AmeriCorps Alums Professional Development Series. Barry is an excellent coach! He is personable, knowledgeable and motivating. While he was volunteering his expertise to the AmeriCorps Alums, you could tell he truly cared for our future and wanted to help each of us produce results. Having experienced Barry's methods and techniques, I would definitely recommend hiring Barry"

Angelina Moya - Manager, Strategy and Support, Chicago Public Schools

"Barry took me on as a client in 1985, when I was looking for a job in tax. I had been out of the tax field for 6 years, pursuing a restaurant business. He showed confidence in my abilities to get back into the technical area of

taxation. And he ultimately placed me in a perfect position. It accelerated my career in the tax field and I will always be thankful for his assistance."

Denise Banachowski - Competent Authority APMA Project Leader

I've worked with Barry on a number of fronts, including recruiter and advisor. He has unparalleled integrity and insight. These attributes are invaluable particularly in these times. I highly recommend Barry to anyone who needs help in finding people and who need career advice. He is straightforward, honest, and helpful. He will make the time for you. And, you can trust him.

Philip P. Moody - Chief Financial Officer at PaxVax, Inc.

"Out of love for his family, his community, and the game of basketball, Barry founded a youth basketball team that I played for. He not only created the team from nothing, but was able to make it wildly successful. In Mighty Ducks-like fashion, he transformed a group of disorganized students who at first couldn't win a game into division champions in just two years. His mentorship allowed each individual to improve to their fullest talents, but he was also very successful at ingraining the idea that the success of the pack mattered most (we were, after all, the Timberwolves).

His leadership skills were acute. Every individual understood their role on the team. Every individual understood that hard work would be required to succeed, and every individual trusted that he knew how to get us there. He was honest always, and encouraging without fail. It was a pleasure knowing him then and it has been a pleasure over the past 15 years getting to know him better"

Raphael Rosen - President at Carbon Lighthouse

"Communication is the key to all relationships. Barry Kleiman is a true communicator who has the ability to teach, lead, and direct groups or individuals towards a common goal, all in a very professional and pleasing manner. His experience as a coach and a mentor to young athletes is a gift for all to share. I consider Barry a friend and colleague and have the highest regard for his abilities. His "love of the game" is not just about basketball. I believe the game for Barry is life."

Bob Trapp - President at American Health & Safety Training, Inc.

Recently, I was fortunate enough to be coached by Barry in an arena in which I had no familiarity. While applying for my first job, Barry provided me with invaluable insight to help guide me through the process. His knowledge of the interview process proved to be instrumental in my efforts. While working with Barry I felt best prepared to showcase all that I have to offer while highlighting the needs of the organization for which I was applying. Learning from Barry gave me the comfort and confidence that I needed to put my best foot forward.

Theo Robertson – Assistant Basketball Coach at University California, Berkeley

Barry has had a tremendous impact on my work ethic, way of thinking and motivation. The time I have had the privilege to spend with him had,, by far, the most efficient and positive influence of discussions with other mentors. If the pounds were the time spent, time spent with Barry is pond for pound the most fruitful and powerful motivation session in the world!

Henri Landes – Lecturer, Author and Consultant on Sustainability

Barry is an inspiration. He has the ability to motivate through conversation and has the ability to provide guidance based on individual needs. Barry is direct, honest and energetic. He has a passion for each individual he comes into contact with and truly wants each person to be successful and happy. He has the unique ability to provide just the right amount of advice and he is a living example of everything he teaches. A true inspiration!

Edward Willett – Vice President, Sponsorship and Topgolf Media

Preface

How This Book Came About

> **"** *Barry, I was very impressed with your enthusiasm &*
> *coaching skills. Men like you served a great need in my life*
> *& I applaud you for your devotion"*
> Dale Brown - Head Coach LSU Basketball

I never...(capitals) N E V E R thought about writing a book until one day while having the honor of lunch with Coach Dale Brown he just asked... *"Barry, did you ever think about writing a book?*

By virtue of intersecting with the lives of Coach Brown's three grandsons while coaching them on the basketball court I was fortunate enough to meet and ultimately be befriended by Coach in 2010.

If you grew up the way I did you'd know why this meeting and befriending was such an amazing honor and privilege...

It was in fact so much of an honor and privilege that yours truly...this near 60 year old man froze while searching for an answer to Coach Brown's question...

"I haven't really Coach but, I'll write a book if you write the Foreword"

"Deal!" said Coach Brown so...

Here I am, several years after our lunch hoping to honor the honor I was given and share with you the reader exactly "How the TRUTH Will Set You and Your Career Free"

The process and purpose of writing a book titled "How the TRUTH Will Set You & Your Career Free" seemed simple enough...

After all, I had been teaching a course by the same name to individuals and groups of 200+ folks since 2006 so how hard could writing a book actually be?

My purpose too was genuine and simple...

Take all of the acquired knowledge that one garners from 70,000 hours on the job and share it with as many people as possible.

It all turned out to be really quite simple too!

Simply a massive undertaking

Simply an enormous test of my organizational skills AND

Simply proving just how naive I was to take on the project

The content parts were far easier to pen as they were a part of my everyday life...multiple times a day for many years but the structure components are quite another story...

This **Preface**, the **Introduction** and much that follows were written again and again and again and again.

I put the whole project on hold for two full years due to my frustration of getting these things and the overall layout to the point where I could hit the PUBLISH button.

Well...through much soul searching and an even greater dose of encouragement from friends, from teachers, from mentors and from Coach Brown's words back at that lunch my book project has taken shape...it's designed to prove to you exactly "How the TRUTH Will Set You & Your Career Free".

Foreword

"I had the opportunity to observe then get to know Barry number of years ago (as he was coaching basketball at an SF Bay Area high school). I became quite impressed with his passion for both the game and for working on the development of young people.

Later in the season we had a chance to have lunch with Barry and continued to be impressed with his intellect, creative ideas, and sincerity, sharing with him at one juncture that he should write a book; it seemed all of those traits would translate to assisting others in their quest to improve their career and overall life opportunities.

He now has completed his book "How The Truth Will Set you And Your Career Free." which is an amalgamation of the past 44 years of his life in the executive search/development world, the book emphasizing again and again that career success begins with being organized, honest, and true to yourself.

I recommend you look into this interesting book, it could be a big help to you."

Dale Brown LSU Head Basketball Coach 1972-1997

" This above all, to thine ownself be true"
Lord Polonius to Laertes, Hamlet - Act 1, Scene 3

Introduction

My name is Barry Kleiman, I've spent the last 44 years of my life learning from, surviving and ultimately thriving in the career success and job search sanity business.

This book is a compendium of those years and is titled as such for the simple reason that there's no one thing I've learned that's more powerful, more scalable, more replicate-able to your career, job search, or overall life, than the TRUTH.

If this seems a cavalier, pretentious or preachy use of those five letters to you (T R U T H), then let's make it even a bit more interesting...let's wager.

I'll bet you the price you paid for this book that if you read on and then apply the TRUTH to every action you take, every statement you make, every thought you have with the whole TRUTH and nothing but the TRUTH as your guide, you'll have discovered the single greatest secret I could possibly share with you for now and forever more!

I'm also willing to bet that the very reason you even sought out a book with this title is that you're in a situation right now in your career or overall life that is rooted somewhere in a lie or stretched TRUTH that you told yourself and/or told another.

"Insanity is doing the same thing over and over and expecting different results"
- Albert Einstein

Here's the deal...if you don't believe in or follow this simply stated path, doesn't matter to me...it's of absolute zero consequence as far as I'm concerned. My life will not change one iota if you keep on doing what you've been doing. Whether or not you change your modus operandi beginning with your mindset will not affect how I live my life.

That said...

If you were to consider what's being offered on the following pages with respect to your overall belief system, then act accordingly...systematically integrating the TRUTH into all you say and do (resumes, cover letters, LinkedIn profile, networking outreach, interviewing etc), then ultimately experience some level of profound positive change(s) in your life...I'd get a great big smile on my face if you wrote me and told me as such!

I'll tell you here what I tell my own children...

"I have no agenda whatsoever for your life...except that you do! As long as it's ethical, moral, legal and nobody gets hurt, you should find a way to construct your life and time living your life ON PURPOSE".

Doing anything else winds up to be in direct conflict with Lord Polonius' admonition to Laertes words and will leave you walking the earth with what is essentially a stone in your shoe...irritating every step you take until an infection of some sort surfaces.

"I'm no hero that's understood"
- Thunder Road, Bruce Springsteen

Before moving on to the actual and specific content of how "The TRUTH Will Set You & Your Career Free" allow me to share a few more of my own TRUTHS for perspective...

My career began way back before office technology even included fax machines...

With all of those years (and with all current modern modes of working removed), comes the experiences and ingenuity needed to have been directly responsible for finding hundreds and hundreds of people viable employment and successfully consulting with hundreds and hundreds more to that same (successful) end.

What may be even more important to share, though, is that those 44 years included 5 huge downturns to the job markets...one of which caused me to essentially go broke along with encountering a resulting level of a near debilitating stress.

I say more important because ultimately, what I learned from it all was that it was **"me"** causing the stress simply by allowing myself to be a victim of and puppet to circumstances!

I was turning into one of the stars in Dr. Spencer Johnson's classic book "Who Moved My Cheese" ...an irritated rat, angry and for a while emotionally paralyzed by the fact that things were not like they used to be...someone or something had indeed "moved my cheese".

Yes, the job market absolutely had its issues and on multiple occasions during my career! Big deal, who cares!!!

What I finally came to realize was that everything each of us really needed for career success and job search sanity (yours truly included) was well within our grasp. All we had to do was simply recognize it for what it was then begin to take action accordingly...look in places other than those we had become accustomed to, and that's the TRUTH!!!

So now...what I endeavor to do, whether with this book, in the programs I teach and/or the private consultations I offer is not to portray myself as a hero of any sort whatsoever, but, as an evangelist for the TRUTH.

The TRUTH is a BRAND

The TRUTH is a STRATEGY

The TRUTH is a MINDSET

By adopting and integrating these things as your own, you'll indeed discover exactly "How the TRUTH Will Set You & Your Career Free".

If you can handle the TRUTH, then turn the page and let's get to it!

TABLE OF CONTENTS

CHAPTER 1

How to W.I.N.

The subtitle of this book speaks to SECRETS of career success and job search sanity. If you have read the INTRODUCTION, then you have already been exposed to SECRET #1...the TRUTH itself.

Perhaps, in your hurry to get to the <u>real</u> secrets shared in these pages, you only glossed over the INTRODUCTION...

If that's the case...PLEASE STOP RIGHT NOW, GO BACK, READ and EMBRACE what's written there as, in and of itself, it may be more important than anything else that follows. I say that for two reasons:

1. *If the concept of the TRUTH resonates with you, then headway has already been made.*

2. *If it (the TRUTH) does not resonate with you, then the rest of what's written here will not work any more than putting regular petrol in a diesel engine...*

Combustion may or may not occur...at best case it will be sporadic. (Which of course is not at all what we're looking to accomplish). Without the TRUTH resonating and resonating to you profoundly my advice would be to go off in search of another way, a better way to get from "A" to "B".

As mentioned in the subtitle, each ensuing chapter contains SECRETS.

They also contain TRUTHS including a bit more about yours truly, told here as it's anecdotal to this chapter's context.

By and large, my career in executive development was an accident...

Not an accident in any sort of bad/train-wreck way...it just did not happen "on purpose". As a result, I spent the better part of 27 years learning then ultimately fixing that fact. This "fix" was for my own sanity/well-being as well as the well-being of anyone who came in contact with me. Regardless of whether you knew me through my work, through my home life, or through my social world, I just became an easier guy to be around!

I finally discovered what was missing through the amalgamation of a few books. One of these books was **The 7 Habits of Highly Effective People** (the other one called **In These Girls Hope is a Muscle**.)

In his book, **The 7 Habits of Highly Effective People**, Dr. Stephen R. Covey taught that all things we humans create are actually created twice...first in your mind, and second in the physical world.

Think of an architect...first drawing a blueprint long before any holes are dug, nails are hammered, etc.

One TRUTH you must understand is...

If you want to attain career success, job search sanity or overall success in your life, you must *create* it in your mind first so as you know yourself today...

What do you want to happen?

Now, you may say something like, *"I've done this before"* or, *"That's not such a SECRET"*.

Well, that's great...you can move forward to some of the other SECRETS that rarely get talked about, but, before you do, let me suggest you asking yourself and answering these three questions:

1. If you have already "heard this before"...are you taking action on what you said you wanted to happen?

2. If you're already taking action...are you taking action to the best of your ability?

3. If you're taking action to the best of your ability...are you doing so consistently, with the highest level of focus and energy within your power?

Remember now...this is what you said YOU wanted to happen.

If you answered "Yes" to these 3 things, I am happy for you! You are way ahead of the game...you get, on a deep, actionable level, both pieces of Dr. Covey's creation model.

Feel free to jump forward to Chapter #3!

If, however, you're not yet fully engaged in knowing what you really want to happen, WHY you want it to happen, and then taking consistent action to do so, let's get back to work... we'll fix that ASAP!

Change is the result of all TRUE learning -

Leo Buscaglia

If you're not acting on/toward what you want to happen then the only option for you to move in the direction of your vision is the word us humans dread the most: CHANGE!

There's a Stanford/MIT educated, MIT lecturer named Peter Senge, who among other things has written a great deal on the subject of CHANGE. I won't go into it all here except to say that Senge stated that the only real way to induce effective CHANGE is to begin with a "brutally honest assessment of your current reality."

Where are you today?

Why are you there?

If you don't start from a place of absolute clarity of your current reality, and you don't tell the TRUTH (the whole truth and nothing but the truth) about it, then the rest of this is going to be that much harder. Again, it will be pointless to go on if this first step is not addressed.

So, let's move the needle on our change with a brutally honest sense of your current reality.

!!!DO THIS PART!!!!

!!!DON'T THINK THIS ISN'T FOR YOU AND JUMP AHEAD TO THE "GOOD STUFF"!!! !!!THIS IS THE "GOOD STUFF"!!!

!!!IF YOU DIDN'T NEED IT, YOU'D BE READING SOMETHING ELSE RIGHT NOW...

...AND THAT MY FRIEND IS THE TRUTH!!!

There are many ways for this "brutally honest assessment of your current reality" to happen...I'll just give you here the one I teach the most...

Write a W.I.N. Statement

W.I.N. is an acronym for **What's Important Now.** It is an inexpensive yet highly effective process to help you organize and gain clarity on your current reality, while also providing a wonderful guide to the moving forward steps needed for what you subsequently want to happen.

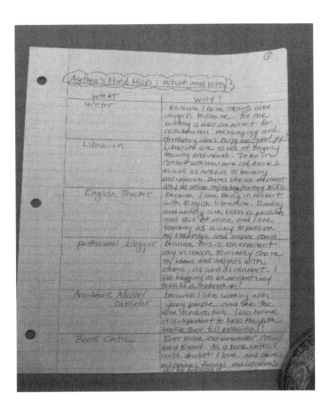

This is a simple way to get started...

Grab a piece of paper and draw a straight line down the middle from top to bottom. On the left side of the line, write WHAT, on the right side of the line write WHY. Then, set the timer on your phone or microwave etc. For 10 minutes, write down every single WHAT you can think of that you deem important to you. I want to encourage you to just write...leave 3-5 lines in between each WHAT, but just keep writing. DO NOT EDIT YOUR DREAMS...there are no wrong WHATS.

When the 10-minute buzzer goes off, STOP, and set your timer for 15 more minutes. Now, on the WHY side of the page, write down exactly that...WHY is each WHAT important to you? If there's not enough room in the space you left in between each item, use another piece of paper. Write until your heart's content or the timer goes off, and then STOP...take a walk...get away from it for a bit.

This is your W.I.N. Statement – What's Important Now to you and WHY. If you're telling yourself the TRUTH, if you're acting on a brutally honest assessment of your current reality, you'll quickly see the areas of your life you should be addressing, first by taking note of the WHAT with the most prolific, robust WHY.

This is not to suggest the other things are not important, relevant, or are not areas you'll want to address. It's just that the W.I.N. Statement will help you attain and stay focused on What's Important Now!!!

I want to suggest a wire-bound notebook simply because you can use it as a journal with your W.I.N. Statement as the opening page(s). You can then refer back to it constantly throughout the change process...the W.I.N Statement acts as a "blueprint" of sorts (in the spirit of Dr. Covey).

An inconvenient TRUTH about all of this is that at least for today...you're not going to satisfy every single one of your WHATS. It won't happen. It can't happen. Take action on your WHATS that have the strongest WHY attached. The stronger your WHY, the stronger your motivation will be to do things.

Allow me please to give you a "Silly, Barry Kleiman Style Analogy" before we move forward.

If I gave you a pick and shovel, and I asked you to dig 4 holes 20 feet deep and 4 feet around, would you do it? I hope the answer is "no" because, I don't know about you but if you've ever dug holes for anything, it's really hard work. There are rocks in the ground. Your pick hits the rocks. It stings your hands. Expletives fly, and you've still got to keep digging. It's hard work. I would not recommend it.

However, WHAT if you wanted to build a home and the only piece of land you could afford to build your home on was at the side of a cliff? What if, in order to make that home stand forever, it needed to have 4 holes at least 20 feet deep and 4 feet around to be filled with concrete? What if I then gave you a pick and a shovel and asked if you would dig those same 4 holes? I hope you'd say, "yes" because now the WHY becomes the fact that you're going to live in that house, and you'll want it to stand forever.

If you want to know exactly where to start your job search, start inside your own mind and start to understand yourself. Start to understand what's important right now and WHY. Start to give yourself a brutally honest assessment of your current reality, and then we can move forward.

Time waits for no one and it won't wait for me..."
Time Waits For No One
-The Rolling Stones

CHAPTER 2

Core Concepts

In the Introduction, we talked about the TRUTH...how those five letters alone are the number one secret that needs be understood and honored for anything worthwhile, and scalable to happen to your career success/job search sanity.

In Chapter One, we discussed Dr. Steven Covey's concept that things are created twice, (once in your own mind and then physically) as well as acquiring a "brutally honest assessment of your current reality" via writing a W.I.N. Statement.

We're about to get started on the physical creation, so please keep these lessons attached to your thoughts and actions as they are critical to all that follows...if you keep a secret to yourself, and/or from yourself, this process will break down immediately.

Before we begin the physical construction phase of building out your job search, I want to encourage you to do yourself an additional favor...don't jump ahead! We're going to work on any number of things but the point of it all is to provide you with a set of tools designed for the purpose of getting you over, around or through the various obstacles and barriers that will inevitably surface as you're getting this (career success and job search sanity) thing constructed.

Variables are one of life's constants...from preconceived notions (some of which may have gotten you to the place you're in right now) to some of the people you'll be interacting with along the way, to changing job market conditions, to potential changes in your personal life...stuff comes up to side-track your thinking and ensuing actions.

It's with that in mind I want to present you the three **Core Concepts** *that TRULY need be built into your psyche, belief system and work plans before we actually start hammering any nails so to speak.*

They are, in my experience and way of thinking, a non-negotiable collection of directional beacons to moving forward with speed, focus, clarity and effectiveness in this career success and job search sanity endeavor!!! (Of course, you can refute or ignore any or all of them, though I can assure you I've tried that for any number of years to far, far less success than heeding them for the past 15).

Core Concept:

An idea of something formed by mentally combining all its characteristics or particulars; a construct

CORE CONCEPT #1 - *MARKETING!!!*

You must become a savvy "Marketeer" when you engage in a job search. It is mission critical!

When I say this, please don't think that you must become one of those hucksters on a late-night infomercial using taglines like:

"But wait, there's more."

"If you call now, you'll get this plus that plus these things...."

TRUTH be told, there is a great deal to learn from these 30-minute sales pitches that we'll discuss moving forward. Another TRUTH is, like them, your job today is unmistakably that of a product marketing whiz... trying to induce someone to pay attention to and hopefully buy what you're offering...it's just in this case, it's you and your skills.

In the next chapters, I'll take you through the process and provide you a short course on marketing, but for now, you need to understand and embrace your new role. Don't slough it off, don't say it's unfair, and don't say, well, my job is a doctor, lawyer, Indian chief or whatever. Your job during this process is, in the most clear and concise way as humanly possible, to make people aware of:

- the value that you provide,

- the manner in which you do it,

- the benefit to them

That's what a marketer does, regardless of the product or service, and that's what you must do for this process to be a winning process for you.

Let's go back to the infomercial for a moment...

You may laugh at them, you may scoff at them, but when they pick up a bowling ball with a vacuum cleaner, they're showing you the strength of their equipment, and of course, what they're trying to prove to you is the benefit to you. When those folks hammer knife handles and cut through aluminum cans with the blades then still slice tomatoes paper thin, they are making a claim, substantiating their claim and proving in the most demonstrative way they possibly can the benefit to you.

If you've seen them and never bought anything, that's fine...the fact that you've seen them (or others for BowFlex, Total Gym, Proactive Skin Care etc.), is because they are on often, and, they are on often for one reason and one reason...their MESSAGE is working!!

Write it down - **Core Concept #1 -** Effective job searches are orchestrated by effective "Marketeers". Again, don't worry about it, if you don't know how you'll learn it in the next chapter.

CORE CONCEPT #2 - Silver Bullets, Shiny Objects, Magic Tricks do not exist.

There are no silver bullets, shiny objects or magic tricks to make this search happen...

If you sincerely believe that you can instantaneously vault yourself into a brand new job because of some new keyword on your resume or some super-duper slick question you asked in an interview, please let me know...I have some beautiful, picturesque swamp land in Florida to sell to you...at a great price too!

As I sit and listen to the YouTube hucksters or LinkedIn prophet tell you about the ten critical interview questions you must know, or the four questions you must ask, I roll my eyes, laugh, and often shout out loud...

"How do they know?

"Do they know the context of the interview?

"Do they want us all to think that every single interview is the same?"

"Are they asking us to believe that every single person on the other side of the desk has the same agenda and the same methodology?"

Really people? *Really?*

There is no one thing...there is no silver bullet, shiny object or magic trick out there that, in and of itself will raise you above the rest. As one of my teachers once said, "If you're looking for magic, go to a magic store."

Make no mistake here...there are certainly better and worse ways to operate and migrate your way around the career success terrain...

That's exactly what we'll be working on. It's based on what I call "consistent authenticity" which can be as powerful as anything you might imagine.

CORE CONCEPT #3 - Systems and Processes kick the crap out of random acts 1,000-1

The antitheses of shiny objects are systems and processes. Systems and processes kick the butt of random acts. Solutions to systemic problems do not occur through haphazard actions.

You cannot lose weight by dieting once a week. You cannot get fit by working out twice a month. There has to be a process to it, there has to be a systemic approach that also fits your ultimate goals. A marathon runner, a world-class athlete has a different set of fitness goals than you or I might make. You have to understand that what you're trying to do is build out a system for your intended goals.

"If you can't describe what you're doing as a process, you don't know what you're doing"

- W. Edwards Demming

This book is all about helping you build a system and make clear for you exactly what you're doing moving forward.

These three core concepts, are both the TRUTH as well as hidden secrets...I highly doubt that you'll see very many people talking about them, yet, they're as powerful as three points of focus you can possibly construe.

If you're still with me, and you still want to begin constructing a better you, let's do so by turning the page and turning you into a "Marketeer".

"Meet the new boss, same as the old boss..." -
Won't Get Fooled Again -
The Who

CHAPTER 3

Marketing

In the last chapter, we talked about the three core concepts that though rarely discussed, are so critical to your success. You must embrace and educate yourself to become a "Marketeer". There is no direct line from A to B, no silver bullets, no shiny objects, no magic tricks. Any good marketing campaign is built around a system...a methodology whose goal is to find effective means to address different people with different pain points, all of which can potentially be solved by what you have to offer.

Military parlance includes a phrase called the "force multiplier effect" which can essentially be defined as follows:

Force multiplication, in military usage, refers to an attribute or a combination of attributes that dramatically increases (hence "multiplies") the effectiveness of an item or group, giving a given number of troops (or other personnel) or weapons (or other hardware) the ability to accomplish greater things than without.

Once you understand the "force multiplication" of a well-constructed marketing campaign systematically rooted in the TRUTH...displaying consistent authenticity at every turn, you'll wonder how else you ever approached the daunting task of seeking refreshed employment.

As mentioned before, I've learned the hard way the problems created by not having a marketing mindset and marketing plan, so in the consultations I offer, the seminars we do, and now within the pages of this book, I want to do my best to stress in reasonable detail what I believe you'll need to know to be effective in your new role of "Marketeer".

I already know you're able, so if you're ready and willing, please allow me to provide you with a "crash course" on marketing.

What I'm about to share is an amalgamation of what I've learned from people like Dan Kennedy and Jay Abraham during the last 15 years. If you haven't heard of either or both of these gentlemen and had the interest to "Google" their names...you'd find out that what I'm about to share is not just informative, but (probably more importantly) incredibly practical for the purposes of you moving forward in your job search, your career, and your life overall. If you pay close attention, I'm guessing that at some point between now and whenever you'll find yourself teaching some of it to your children and/or anyone else in your life who you're seeking to help.

Learn this content now...you'll forever be armed with tools that 99.9% of the job seeking world will never know, plus, as an added bonus, you'll keep your sanity all along the way.

Challenge yourself to think like a "Marketeer" ...your new job. You won't regret it!!

At its very core...marketing is conveying value!

There are other explanations to make the term clear, but that one, due to it's simplicity has always worked for me with no other real explanation needed!

*I mentioned this before and will do so again...if you want to see "conveyed value" at one of its most familiar, most effective forms, go onto YouTube, search for and watch some of the highest grossing infomercials ever produced. These are items that have sold hundreds and hundreds of millions of dollars' worth of product all using some very similar formulas...doing all they possibly can to **not just talk** about "melting away fat" or "setting and forgetting" but **more importantly, tangibly conveying the value they provide to the potential buyer**.*

From the Total Gym to the Thigh Master, from Snuggie's to the Showtime Rotisserie, the list goes on and on...each promotion doing their very best to demonstratively answer the question "why them?" Why would you or anyone buy their product or service instead of another's?

If this seems too abstract, let me bring it home right in your face...

Why you?

Why would the person on the "other side of the desk" choose you vs. any other option they have...including not hiring anyone at all?

When you endeavour out into the oft-time harrowing world of employment transition, your job is to understand and make readily available the answer(s) to that question. (As an aside, this is the TRUTH even if you're looking to change jobs inside of your current company.)

So... if marketing is conveying value and you need to be the most effective conveyor possible then you need to understand the science of human behavior a bit...

BUT WAIT...THERE'S MORE!

As sorry as I am to tell you the following, it is in fact the TRUTH...

Quite often, the best "conveyor" of value beats out the best "purveyor" of similar or even lesser value to the finish line.

This sucks, right?

Here you are, a highly skilled person of your craft being beaten out by a person who may know or do less, but is far better versed in conveying what they do know.

Again...this is the TRUTH which I really hope you get because I'm now going to keep this crash course moving along so we can make sure this doesn't ever happen to you.

You have value to convey...I am sure of that!

I am also sure that your ability/methodology for getting the word out there in an ongoing, effective, authentic fashion is hardly your strength.

The reason I know this? Easy...if you were great at conveying, you wouldn't be reading this right now!

You might be reading other chapters, brushing up on other search process components, but you wouldn't be questioning the acumen required for your new Chief Marketeer job and it's the foremost goal...marketing yourself!

But I digress and want to move on...

Marketing methodology has three specific, intertwined components

1. What's your **MESSAGE?**

2. Who's your **MARKET?**

3. What's the best **MEDIA** to get your **MESSAGE** to your **MARKET?**

GREAT MESSAGE - WRONG MARKET

In the early iteration of my search career, I would bang my head hard and repeatedly up against the proverbial wall of the gatekeeper…

Even if I was representing a candidate with wonderful credentials, whose experience would seemingly work "hand in glove" with a specific company's needs, it was very tough to get through the door.

In those early days of my career, personnel managers, and human resource folks really wanted nothing to do with what I was selling. I have made some great friends with many, many folks in that area of business but back then, not so much…they had their own sources, their own ways of doing things, their own ego, their own pride and until you established a relationship that proved there was something in it for them, they would rarely pick up the phone.

To reference something we discussed earlier with respect to your W.I.N Statement, their WHY was not strong enough for them to take action.

RIGHT MESSAGE - RIGHT MARKET - WRONG MEDIA

The **RIGHT MARKET** is almost always the individual with the most compelling WHY. Said differently, the **RIGHT MARKET** is many times the person with the most important problem to solve…the largest "pain point" to alleviate etc. (e.g. Selling ice to

Eskimos on a cold Alaskan day in January may not be a market with a pain point that more ice will solve).

Anecdotal to your job search...

If you were fortunate enough to find out the name of the person hiring for a specific position, you would then more than likely have the **RIGHT MARKET** (you'd still need the **RIGHT MEDIA** to get to that person as they too have gatekeepers but more on that next).

Back in those same early days of my search career this too happened often; I had the **RIGHT MESSAGE** (a great candidate, great resume, great background overall), knew the company had a specific need for someone with those skills (aka **MARKET**), but then needed the **RIGHT MEDIA** to get the **MESSAGE** to that **MARKET**.

This involved any number of **MEDIA** methods including actions such as: calling the **RIGHT MARKET's** direct phone number after hours (so as to avoid the gatekeeper), and/or sending that same person a Special Delivery envelope marked "PERSONAL and CONFIDENTIAL", and/or sending books, boxes of chocolate etc. each of which also contained a letter explaining why I went to such lengths and, of course, a copy of the candidate's resume.

When you go into job search mode...guess what? You're fighting these exact same battles! So...

Moving forward, we're going to explain HOW TO...

- Build your authentic, TRUTH based **MESSAGE**,

- Find the **MARKETS** that you want to access

- Decide out the correct **MEDIA** form(s) for you to do so.

I understand if this all sounds daunting, as that's often the case with most things any of us never really studied, worked on and polished. However, when we build out your system you'll have what is in essence a "paint-by-numbers process for it all, then be empowered to act with great confidence as you'll have the tremendous power of the TRUTH on your side.

Have you given serious consideration about your **MESSAGE** lately? Let's do that next...

Flip the page!

> *Tinker, tailor, soldier, sailor, rich man, poor man, beggar man, thief,*
> *Or what about a cowboy, policeman, jailer, engine driver, or a pirate chief?*
> *Or what about a ploughman or a keeper at the zoo,*
> *Or what about a circus man who lets the people through?*
> *Or the man who takes the pennies on the roundabouts and swings,*
> *Or the man who plays the organ or the other man who sings?*
> *Or what about the rabbit man with rabbits in his pockets*
> *And what about a rocket man who's always making rockets?*
> *Oh it's such a lot of things there are and such a lot to be*
> *That there's always lots of cherries on my little cherry tree."*

Now We Are Six

-A.A. Milne

CHAPTER 4

Your Message

In Chapter 3 - Marketing, we discussed the fact that at its simplest form, marketing is conveying value and that effective marketing has three distinct yet synergistic components:

- A well-reasoned, well-stated **MESSAGE**

- The correct **MARKET** in which to place that **MESSAGE**

- The ideal form of **MEDIA** so that **MESSAGE** can reach that **MARKET**

In an attempt to demystify all of this and make it seem far less daunting, let's begin building our message with several extremely hi-tech, highly expensive tools...

Grab a stack of **3 x 5 index cards** and **several sharpened pencils...**

On these cards, write down what you really would like to do with your work. (For each different thought, please use a separate card).

Rich Man, Poor Man, Beggar Man, Thief, Doctor, Lawyer, Indian Chief...whatever it is you are considering, whatever areas in which you'd like to work...write it down on a card.

Do yourself a favor...try not to use titles. Instead, on the front of each index card, simply write your area of functional expertise. And then, on the back of the corresponding card, use bullet points to explain just how your understanding of that particular expertise benefits the end user.

I CANNOT STRESS HOW IMPORTANT DOING THIS IS TO EVERYTHING ELSE THAT WE'LL COVER MOVING FORWARD!!!!

If you're a very talented corporate accountant, well versed in the areas of debits and credits, etc. state Corporate Accountant on the front of your card. On the back, state how your expertise benefits the folks who receive your work.

Why am I asking you to do this? You might be saying "I already know what I do".

Do you? Really and TRULY?

When was the last time you really thought through all of what you do, all of whom it best serves, how it best serves them in great detail and depth? If you've done all of these things and written them down, you're ready to move on from this chapter...

If you haven't, or need a refresher, I'm urging you to get to work on those index cards!

In order for you to optimize what you have to offer, you must first be certain you understand it on as deep a level as exists.

As an aside...

Just yesterday I was speaking with a client/friend who is in the business of cosmetic sales, and uses an MLM model to build her business. We discussed the products she was selling but we also spoke IN DEPTH about the benefits to the end user.

"Lipstick does far more than add color to one's lips; it also provides moisturizing to the user's lips which produces a healthier glow, which in turn provides the person with a bit more confidence in their personal presentation, which in turn makes it easier for that person to feel more at ease/less self-conscious when making presentations, which gives them more opportunities to meet more people, which in turn offers more opportunities to network and build their business, which in turn would afford them greater odds at deriving the income they desire to support their family etc., etc."

Scoff if you will, but every single word of that is the TRUTH for a large, large percentage of folks who buy beauty products! Think about the many benefits of what you offer and just how you'd build it into your **MESSAGE.**

What I'm asking you to do here, at the end of the day, is **have a greater amount of self-respect for all that you know and do!**

Just so we're clear here...I am not talking about misplaced arrogance either...I'm talking about the confidence stemming from the TRUTH of knowing that who you are and how what you know matters at a far deeper level than many people often give themselves credit for.

Think about it...tell the TRUTH but tell the WHOLE TRUTH.

You don't need to place a higher value on what you provide, but if you TRULY are interested in career success and job search sanity you should consider doing so.

"How the TRUTH Will Set You & Your Career Free" **SECRET:**

As you're compiling your bullet point lists, don't just settle for the first benefits that spring to mind...those are often surface benefits and of course, write those down, but go a bit deeper. After you write down your first bulleted list of benefits, ask yourself, "What does this benefit ultimately do for someone?" By questioning each of your "surface level" benefits, you can drill deeper and deeper into the core value of what you have to offer. For example, a surface benefit might be: I am excellent at Excel or PowerPoint. Great, that's fantastic. Now let's drill deeper. What else does someone else get from your proficiency with Excel and PowerPoint etc? Be as specific and in depth as you possibly can...you know your work at a far deeper level than most...not sharing it is selfish!!

Please remember my admonition about titles...DO NOT worry about titles YET. We're trying to draft a powerful message and that message should never be something such as: "I want to be a C level executive."

There's no reason for anybody to pay attention to that yet! You have to provide the value first; you have to get people's attention first. I would warn with you that a titled-laden message... is a bad message.

"How the TRUTH Will Set You & Your Career Free" SECRET:

Bad **MESSAGES** almost never get good jobs!

I'll close this chapter by showing off some of my speed reading skills and now read you a very powerful book...in than less than 180 seconds!

The book is called *The Irresistible* Offer it's written by a gentleman named Mark Joyner.

In his book, Joyner says that, whenever two people come together to do business of any sort, a tape begins whirring through the listener's mind (I guess in this day and age, it's a digital device, but regardless). The device clicks on as an immediate reflex to any sales pitch, and it's programmed to have the brain ask itself these four questions:

1. What are you selling?

2. What's it going to cost me?

3. Why should I believe you?

4. What's in it for me?

Continuing on, Joyner teaches that if your proposal answers those four questions pre-emptively...before they ever have a chance to get asked by the listener, you will have made a very powerful proposal!

If, on the other hand your proposal does not answer those questions, the listener will either stop listening or listen only minimally...neither of which are in your best interests, obviously!

You have to have the right **MESSAGE**, and if those four questions are answered in your **MESSAGE** you are on the right track. For it to be effective, it must contain as many benefits to the end user as possible with as little points of doubt possible.

OK...my 180 seconds are up!

We've gotta go find the **MARKET** for your awesome **MESSAGE,** so let's keep going...

Hopefully you're reading each chapter to its conclusion...there's a vital "How the TRUTH Will Set You & Your Career Free" **SECRET** *relating to "Win-Win" toward the end of the next one!!!!*

" *Do you love me? I can really move!"*
"Do you love me? I'm in the groove!"
"Do you love me? Now that I can dance!"

Do You Love Me?
-The Contours

CHAPTER 5

Finding A Market

e've discussed in the last two chapters the fact that:

MARKETING is simply conveying value and for it to be effective, we must have...

The right **MESSAGE** and get that to...

The right **MARKET** using...

The right **MEDIA** to do so!

As we move along through the nuances of that model, we discussed in the last chapter how to construct an effective **MESSAGE** and will now begin to talk about finding a **MARKET.**

A quick but not so subtle reminder here...

We are building a system, and as in any system worthy of its flow chart, the total is greater than the sum of the parts, so circling back to the bedrock of our system, I wanted to be sure you keep in mind its **Core Concepts**.

Why am I bringing this reminder up now?

Core Concept #1 - MARKETING!!

Hopefully you recall my continuous urging in our last chapter about making a deeper dive into your **MESSAGE (**after all, it was just in the last chapter **:-))...**

So, you should recall the reason for this urging; I wanted you to dive deeper and deeper into your **MESSAGE** so that it became as clearly stated, well-reasoned, benefit laden as possible!!!

MORE BENEFITS = BROADER APPEAL
BROADER APPEAL = EXPANDED SIZE OF POTENTIAL
MARKET

All of which of course is the goal of any astute "Marketeer"...

Here are two easily verified, tangible examples ...

EXAMPLE #1

Oakland, California is home to "Clorox Corporation".

My guess is that you and almost every single person you know has, at one point or another in their life, used or at least know of their flagship product "Clorox Bleach".

At its very essence, this flagship product is common household bleach: NaClO.

*Clorox via textbook usage of the **MESSAGE, MARKET, MEDIA** model took this NaClO formula (which could easily be replicated by a "B" average high school chemistry student) and developed it into a worldwide brand, a household name!*

The product they produced was a simple chemistry formula...it can still be made by countless individuals...nothing really proprietary.

*It was only when they drilled down further...into the all of the benefits of NaClO, that their transformation as a company occurred. They were now able to build a **MESSAGE** clearly describing those multiple values for the end-user which, in turn, **made the entire world their MARKET**.*

The NaClO concoction was in essence the easy part, positioning it in numerous ways to create a multi-billion dollar, internationally acclaimed company was the genius.

EXAMPLE #2

(I copied and pasted the following directly from the ARM & HAMMER website...this is their **MESSAGE!)**

Sure, you know our little orange box. But did you know that for more than 165 years, people have chosen pure, versatile, effective, safe, and affordable ARM & HAMMER™ Baking Soda for baking, household, and personal care uses. With countless uses for about $1, no other product does more throughout your home.

"Pure, versatile, effective, safe, affordable FOR baking, household and personal care uses...Countless uses for about $1...no other product does more throughout your home"

They also have a Solutions Guide on their website...going deeper and deeper into all of the uses around the home, This guide goes to great lengths to discuss how their product can be used with babies, with pets, for cleaner skin for easier digestion etc., etc., etc.

There's a near limitless number of reasons to buy Arm & Hammer Baking Soda...good for them! Great VALUE CONVEYANCE!

At the end of the day, Arm & Hammer Baking Soda is - just pure sodium bicarbonate. (They do use a chemical reaction process through which trona ore is mined, then heated until it turns into soda ash, but this is hardly proprietary technology!)

What it is though is a great **MESSAGE** through which a HUGE **MARKET** was built!

35

The smart purveyor is one able to truly understand the depth of what they have to offer so they can then become the brilliant (and highly successful) conveyor of value.

This is exactly what I want for you!

Those most frustrated in their careers and suffering from a bad case of job search INSANITY are those who look at themselves as "JUST ANOTHER".

Clorox and Arm & Hammer are really just another set of simple to construct products that via great **MARKETING,** have become iconic in their fields!!

Ultimately, this book is asking you to seek deeper and deeper TRUTHS about many things not the least of which are ALL that you have to offer.

I am on one knee right now BEGGING YOU to not think of yourself as

"Just another _____!"

The sad, sad part is that most people don't value themselves enough to take the time to think this way or to take action on their thinking...

The reason the 1% is the 1% is simply that they've placed a higher value on what they bring!

Remember, career success and job search sanity are complex problems that cannot be solved with silver bullet, shiny object, magic trick solutions!

Do your absolute best to think of yourself and the value you can provide with as broad a brush as TRULY possible...the **MARKET** available to you will then expand with every stroke of your brush!!!!

Onward with a bit more calibration in our quest to define and find a **MARKET...**

In this era of social media, online job boards, LinkedIn, good old-fashioned conversation etc. there really are clues to the **MARKET** everywhere. It should be noted here that there is a *hidden job market* (which can often be discovered by piecing together clues found on social media!)

Monster Board, CareerBuilder, LinkedIn and the like are all obvious, reasonable places to begin...HOWEVER, there are ways we'll broach to leverage what you learn in these places to a much greater potential advantage than what's being said on the surface of these portals!

Another great place to find a **MARKET** is with people you know.

They might work for a company you're targeting or know someone who does.

If you really just want to work for this or any specific type of company, or in a certain type of industry, then be clear about

WHY (how that fits into your priorities) then develop a **MESSAGE** to clearly present it to another. If it's not clear to the other side...the chances of it being effective or hitting home are about the same as a soap bubble's chance to survive in a meat-grinder.

If there is a company that fits your profile, whether or not you see a job posted there should be of little consequence to your efforts.

Your job as "Marketeer" is to find a way (a form of **MEDIA** to reach out to that company with your **MESSAGE.** There are multiple ways to do this of course...including just asking a person you might know who works at the company or knows a person that does...after all asking is a form of **MEDIA** yes?

There is always the possibility that you don't know a soul who works at a targeted company or know someone who knows someone. No sweat! If you genuinely want to explore opportunities in that company there are other forms of **MEDIA** to get your **MESSAGE** to the **MARKET** which we'll discuss moving forward in the next chapter.

!!!CAUTION!!!!

It's imperative that I remind you again that we're building a methodology here where each part connects and builds on the integrity of the other. Any "ask" you make has to be the right type of "ask"...it must be built around the 4 points laid out earlier when I "read" Mark Joyner's *The Irresistible Offer* to you.

To reiterate...some **MARKETS** are obvious such as on the job boards, on corporate websites, on LinkedIn, etc. but there are many jobs that will not be found on any job board anywhere.

Believe it or not...one the main reasons they won't be found is that nobody (including you) ever brought a **MESSAGE** to the **MARKET** that satisfied somebody's need to the point where they couldn't live without what was being presented...and that is the TRUTH plain and simple!

Every one of us, at one time or another has gone to a retail store and come home with things that weren't necessarily on our list. Something happened in that store that caused a buying reaction at that time that may not have been there until...well, until it was.

You may think that hiring is not necessarily done that way, and while certainly not all is, the TRUTH is that much hiring is in fact done exactly that way.

At a bare minimum of 50% of the jobs I've filled in my forty-four years, were jobs that weren't posted anywhere publicly! These included:

- *Jobs that weren't open ever at all*

- *Jobs that had been open but were closed because an appropriate candidate could not be found*

- *Jobs that came open due to someone or someone's spouse relocating etc., etc.*

The fact was that we were able to craft a compelling enough **MESSAGE** *to the company to make things happen. Right place at the right time? Sure, there is that possibility, however, there is zero traction on any hiring until the* **MESSAGE** *matches the* **MARKET.**

(Who would have thought that the same product that one used as a leavening agent for your cookies could also be used to cure indigestion, or whiten your teeth? Arm & Hammer, that's who!)

"How the TRUTH Will Set You & Your Career Free" - Career Success and Job Search Sanity Secret:

As you go out defining an appropriate **MARKET**, you must keep YOU in mind!

There has to be a benefit to you in all of this as well!

Remember your W.I.N Statement!!

If you're providing ditch digging services to someone who needs thousands of those dug, that's great for them. If you have to dig those same ditches manually, and you wind up breaking your back there's no real "Win-Win", and there must be a "Win-Win' if you expect career success and job search sanity.

I realize fully well that there are economic realities...

I realize we all need to eat, pay rent etc., though, if you have a humble but definite respect for yourself, you will make each career decision a means to an end. If you take that job as a ditch digger, it should be because it's either the only job available right now and your flat broke OR you have your eyes on eventually owning 10-20 Bobcats that dig ditches with powered shovelling.

If there's not a "Win-Win", if the job you take does not have a built-in means to an end, you're going to walk around every day with yet another stone in your shoe. (As Aesop's fable went, you're going to kill the goose that laid the golden egg.)

The **MARKET** is everywhere. You need to open your eyes and your ears and not just accept for verbatim if you don't see a specific job in a company that you'd like to work for.

Sometimes you have to make your own **MARKET**.

And I know this again could be daunting, but we're going to talk about different **MEDIA** forms in the next chapter to get your **MESSAGE** to the **MARKET**. Let's go!

CHAPTER 6

Media

The last chapter's goals were about getting you to consider all avenues for defining then finding a **MARKET** or two for your **MESSAGE.** What was also stressed was for you to use your imagination so you're not just looking at the obvious sources but for discovering all of the possible entities that could benefit from the value you provide.

Also discussed/reiterated was the critical nature of your TRUTHFULLY crafted, clearly stated, well-reasoned, as benefit laden as possible **MESSAGE.** It's being reiterated because of the power of a strong message...the stronger it is, the more attached to it you'll become...the more attached to it you become, the more committed you'll be to churn more possibilities through your mind. All of this chain will ultimately raise the chances of you finding the role or at least a path to the role you most desire.

In this chapter, we're going to discuss how to best get that **MESSAGE** delivered to the correct **MARKET**.

In this modern era, most folks resort/default to email. As terrible an idea as this is in and of itself, those folks are frankly far better off than the ones who simply default to submitting resumes to job boards and hoping for the best.

In the spirit of a little bit of fun here's a pop-quiz of sorts on what we've covered thus far.

Ready?

OK! More often than not, the prevailing wisdom is that one's resume is the most important part of a job search, (to some, maybe the only part). So think about your resume and answer this: Is your resume the **MESSAGE** or the **MEDIA** taking your **MESSAGE** to the **MARKET**, or both?

So we can keep this train moving, let's for the time being call it **MEDIA**.

What are some of the other forms of **MEDIA** to get your **MESSAGE** to the **MARKET**?

Your LinkedIn profile?

Your cover letter?

Blog posts? (If you're so ambitious...and I suggest you should be so ambitious).

Responding to LinkedIn posts made by other people?

Talking to people? (Old school **MEDIA)**

There are a lot of ways to do this, but most importantly, please don't ever assume that (in and of itself) because you electronically send your resume to a job board or company website that you are acting with a great deal of respect for all that you are and have to offer!

*Please know that by no means am I trying to knock any of these things. Each of them are a form of **MEDIA,** but don't ever assume that if you sent your resume electronically to twenty places today that you're conducting an effective job search or acting responsibly in your role as Marketeer.*

"Hope is not a strategy"

- James Cameron

Perhaps one of the single greatest secrets you can learn from this entire book is that electronic submission of your resume is in and of itself one of the worst things you can do!

Why? Simply because it could work!

The TRUTH is that it could, but 99 times out of 100 it won't, and you'll be walking around with hope and only hope as a strategy.

What's a better strategy?

Well, that depends on how much you honor yourself.

How much do you value your time?

How much do you honor the commitments you've made (implicitly or explicitly) to your family?

How much do you value your sanity?

If on a scale 1-10 scale with 10 being the top, your answer is 10, then you'd realize you need to take every possible means to get your **MESSAGE** to the right **MARKET**.

Remember the "force multiplier effect"? Try every means possible... have no concern which mode accesses the target...

*The TRUTH is, when you begin to consider what **MEDIA** approach will work best, you actually have no idea. Unless you possess some psychic abilities of significant inside information as to which of the many modalities available to each of us is most effective to get your **MESSAGE** to the right **MARKET**...try them all!*

"Constant dripping hollows out a stone."
— **Titus Lucretius Carus**

Remember, this is your life, your livelihood, your career so try any and all of these or combinations of them!

- Email may be fine

- Personal connection may be fine

- Phone calls may be fine (particularly if it's after hours when gatekeepers have gone home and you can access your **MARKET** directly!)

- Snail mail letters may be fine

- Cover letters and resumes sent in Fed Ex-like envelopes may be fine

- Standing outside a company's headquarters with a resume in your hand may be fine

- Putting grabbers in your handwritten addressed envelopes along with your resume and cover letter may be fine

(A grabber is a three dimensional something that goes inside of the envelope so when somebody feels it, they wonder what it is and often feel curious/compelled to open it.)

Sending any and all types of communication are beyond fine...all depending if you really score a "10" in our little test above!

You may be saying what almost everybody says to me when I offer this mindset:

"Barry, won't it seem like I'm just badgering and annoying people?"

The TRUTH is... possibly "yes".

The people who have no interest or need may very well feel badgered and/or annoyed, the same way each of us usually feel when called, emailed or contacted in some way by a person marketing a proposition of their own.

That said, I want you to do three things:

1. Consider again the fact that this is your life, your time, your career, your family...

2. Go back once again and read your W.I.N Statement...read through your WHYS. WHY are you trying to do WHAT you're trying to do? No WHY = no committed action.

3. Read through your **MESSAGE** again...is it strong, is it compelling...does it speak the TRUTH about the value you bring? Seek the TRUTH...speak the TRUTH...it will set you free AND drive you forward!

Let me provide a bit more perspective here so you don't just think I'm some psycho, pit-bull type of personality. (If you were to go on my LinkedIn profile and read through the various recommendations people have been kind enough to write, you'd find in fact the exact opposite to be the TRUTH)

"How the TRUTH Will Set You & Your Career Free" NUGGET -

There's a significant amount of science at work in any successful product marketing campaign and because a product marketing campaign is what we're building here with your job search, we must understand and implement a bit of that science.

Allow me to explain a bit...

Science has shown that it takes up to seven impressions to make a sale.

It's been proven that people take 6 visits to an automobile dealership before they make a purchase.

Think about the commercials you hear on the radio...the phone number to call to get more information on whatever product is being repeated 4...5...6 times. "That's 1-800-222-2222. 1-800-222-2222. 1-800-222-2222" The folks authoring successful promotions understand the importance of the science involved, and so should you!

This science is a reality!

This is why when people don't know, don't understand, don't accept or don't execute in conjunction with this scientific TRUTH in mind, they default to things like ONLY writing a resume or ONLY sending it to a the job boards or ONLY reaching out to someone who they think is a personal connection. As you've probably experienced, more often than not these "ONLY" methods hit roadblocks far more often than not and usually find the job-seeker in a state of futility, frustration, often times, giving up!

Your marketing campaign has to take into account the force multiplier effect. You have to try any and every **MEDIA** modality to get your **MESSAGE** to the **MARKET**.

"Our greatest weakness lies in giving up. The most certain way to succeed is always to try just one more time."
- Thomas Edison

Once again...you're only going to do this if it's TRULY important to you, if your WHY outweighs your fear.

Your WHY is what keeps you focused.

Your WHY is what eliminates the "drift effect".

People who are willing to keep pushing are almost always those with a strong WHY and those are the people who wind up getting over the hump.

Resilience is one of the most important attributes you can possess.

I'll say this once again to stress a point...I have decades of experience getting people jobs, crafting **MESSAGES**, finding **MARKETS**, inventing and applying any number of **MEDIA** options for getting past gatekeepers.

I've made my living doing so.

I've put my kids through college with my ability to do so.

I'm not bragging...I'd say it was never easy...I absolutely learned the hard way...what's being shared here is to make it easier for you!

We're about to get into some of the specific tools that are all a part of your campaign, but first, I want to stress...

Your WHY must outweigh your fear of executing on all that you just read. Without this, there's very little that can help you take control of your own career success and job search sanity.

Without this SECRET, you'll see that while important, things such as your resume alone are really a near ineffective tool. This book is all about solving problems systematically as opposed to haphazardly.

In our next chapter, we're going to start to talk about some of these things that you can do to make your marketing more effective:

- Networking

- LinkedIn Profile

- Cover Letters

- Resumes

- Interviewing and beyond (and the beyond is REALLY IMPORTANT!!!)

" Connection, I just can't make no connection.
But all I want to do is to get back to you."

Connection
-The Rolling Stones

CHAPTER 7

The Truth About Networking

I *decided to use a transcription of the NETWORKING segment of a Career Development seminar I was teaching. It was such a wonderful experience overall and the feedback from those in attendance provided me with the confidence that the MESSAGE component of this particular segment was a good one...not just because of my answers, but because of the questions asked.*

One last thing here, anecdotal to the very first question "What exactly is networking" ...it very much can be and really should be a form of MEDIA to help you get your MESSAGE to the MARKET.

Question: What exactly is networking? It seems like I am just using people...

Barry: Great question...great first question actually!

I have a strong dislike for the term NETWORKING if for no other reason than the fact that it makes people feel like they are (in your words) "using people". I really believe that networking should be thought of more as **connecting** than of using people.

How can you add value to someone else's life? How can you learn about somebody? How can you literally connect with somebody? If you just go in ... it's a little bit like dating. If when you first meet somebody your only interests are carnal pursuits or something like that, you have the wrong mindset as far as networking is concerned. If you can connect with people on a level where the connection is genuine, you'll find great value in doing so. You'll find great value in being able to get to know about somebody.

I believe networking is connecting, I believe you want to start with a **listen first** mentality. Listen and understand who these people are, what they like, what they like to talk about.

Does that help at all?

Question: What is its importance and what role does it play?

Barry: Another great question! Let me answer it first with a phrase that I heard once before...I didn't make it up, but have ripped it off continually as it answers your question profoundly. "Your network is your net worth!"

How that manifests specifically here...within the context of the overall is if in fact you have the mindset that I talked about as far as the overall job search is concerned, it can be one of your "marketing arms. (I'm going to add the MEDIA channels to this text) It's a marketing arm because, again, if you understand that marketing is conveying value, here's a way where you have a chance in any type of conversation to show your value. Maybe not your technical value, but your value as a human being!

We all like to do business with people we know, like, and trust. It is your opportunity to get somebody to know you, hopefully to like you, and hopefully to trust you.

Networking done with a "Win-Win" mindset, a "connecting" mindset has the potential to provide potential social proof of who you are. Do you hold doors for people? How do you act? Do you talk out of turn? All these things are part of your networking and you need to understand it. Networking could also reveal employment opportunities that are not available to the naked eye, to the general public. Many jobs go unadvertised. If you wind up talking to somebody who is connected to a certain job in a certain company, they may know that their boss or their boss's boss have a job that they've been thinking about, but never made public.

Essentially, what it has the potential to do is to shorten the string of the job search process in a perfect world. The last thing I'll say about the "importance" it plays is this... in a job search, you are, unlike in our society, guilty until proven innocent. People look at you, "I wonder why he or she is looking. What's wrong with them?" This provides you an opportunity to dispel some level of that doubt simply by being a good, genuine person during your networking.

Question: What are the best places to network?

Barry: Well... "Barry Kleiman 101" has a dogma attached that says you're always interviewing. I believe that deeply, and I also deeply believe you're always networking too. Again, do you hold doors for people? Are you curious in social situations? Do you say thank you to the people who serve you coffee in the morning? Are you curious if you're in cab? Are you curious and sensitive about the people around you, because whether you like it or not, you're always networking. People are always observing you.

I'll tell you a story about a gentleman who I helped...I coached and counseled at one point during his career. This sounds like an episode to a TV show or something but it's a very true story...

This client was sitting in a Starbucks in Sunnyvale, California and the CEO of a very large, multi-billion-dollar company walked by him... tripped over, and as a result, spilled coffee in the lap of my client. So, this guy had hot coffee spilled in his lap. Of course, the person who spilled it was very embarrassed and couldn't apologize enough and ultimately gave him, the guy who got the coffee spilled on his lap, his card and offered to pay whatever damages incurred.

Today, my client is an executive vice president of the company where the CEO works. He handled himself so well under the pressure that he wound up working for these people and found a huge job. Granted, he had to be competent in his work, but he never would have gotten there if he didn't understand that networking is conveying value. Grace under fire...

Plain and simply stated...you're always networking!

Question: Who are the best people to have in my network?

Barry: Well, I'll say again what I said before (I told you I use it continually), your network is your net worth. Bottom line. At the end of the day that's the TRUTH and if you're TRULY intelligent you'll treat it as such.

The best connections are the best network components. I said this too before, but I'm going to say it again, we all like to do business with people we know, like, and trust. The best people to have in your network are people who you connect with the best. There's no point in having a big network of people who you haven't connected with at all.

For many years I used a program called ACT as my CRM...this is before cloud based packages existed and back in those days my database of people had 8,529 records. In this database were their names, addresses, name of their employer (last we spoke), at least one telephone number and often email addresses. Now, that's quite a bit of contact information which might make one think these folks were a part of my network...

I'd be lying through my teeth and could not with a straight face tell you I was "connected" to all those people, so, at some level, they're not really my network. They were just names in a database. Your best networks are your best connections.

Question: What's an ideal size of network?

Barry: I hate to repeat myself, but in some sense, I'll answer this question about the size of network with a similar answer to the one we just had (about best people to have in your network). I get these questions all the time. Once again, I don't know if there's an ideal size. I think the idea is that connecting is the key. The size of your network, to me, is not particularly relevant. It could be very small. It could be larger. If you don't stay in touch...if you don't continually stay connected, then there would be a problem with the effectiveness of that connection.

There are many ways to form an effective network of people which we will talk about at a deeper level, but you should just know that the size of your network is the number of people you can constantly, consistently, authentically stay in touch with. Staying connected is a process and a critical mission. The size of your network has a lot to do with how many people you can stay connected with at some genuine level.

Question: Can you give me tips for a natural network?

Barry: Oh man...I'm about to sound like a broken record (or maybe for you folks a skipping CD). Networking is really connecting. First and foremost, you need to be a great listener. Dr. Steven Covey in his amazing book, The 7 Habits of Highly Effective People, stated in one of the habits...I don't remember which one of the seven...maybe 5th or 6th to "seek first to understand, then to be understood" this habit alone can change your entire life. As an aside, if you haven't read that book it's a MUST...I have read it several times and it remains on my desk as a reference manual...the only thing I don't like about it is that I didn't write it!

Be a great, great listener...

You also want to be informed about current events...

You want to be observant...there are clues everywhere...

If you're shy, smiling is no sin... You want to look approachable as opposed to being in the corner all grouchy and grumpy...

You want to have a good intro to a conversation. You want to have a good out-tro to a conversation. These are just things that if you have in your mind and you've talked about them, you can gracefully enter and gracefully exit conversations.

It's a plus for you if you are a voracious reader or a person who is quite knowledgeable on a broad scope of issues, so that when conversations occur, you will be able to maneuver your way through and deliver convincingly to your listeners should the opportunity arise...this is where the listening can really help...is there any opportunity or are you just blurting out of context to what's actually happening? Be wise with your words; don't over-talk so that you don't start boring your listeners.

Again, networking is staying connected, but don't be boring.

Question: What's the single best technique, if any?

Barry: Well, I'd say that the TRUTH is the best technique possible. The TRUTH if you know something...the TRUTH if don't know something...the TRUTH if you're just walking into a conversation...uninvited as it were; "I couldn't help but noticing that you guys seemed to be having a very entertaining conversation and couldn't resist coming over to listen...please tell me if that's not OK" kind of a thing.

Personally, I'm a person who believes in paying forward first. I'm not new to that obviously... I think you've heard it before. Remember, everything you do has to pay homage to the fact that you are an authentic human being...if you can accomplish that, the world will be your oyster. It may take a bit longer to have your credibility deemed credible, but once you've shown "consistent authenticity" with all that you do, you will join the 0.05% of the world. There are some people who will try to take advantage of this for sure but even then...this is another example of exactly "How the TRUTH Will Set You & Your Career Free"...you'll quickly learn who the givers in your life are as well as who the takers are. Don't let the latter influence how you act or behave, simply remove them from your life.

Raise your hand if you've ever seen a movie call "A Bronx Tale"...Robert De Niro plays a bus driver, Chazz Palminteri as a local neighborhood gangster type... it might be before your time...in any case, De Niro has a son who he's trying to teach to be an upstanding citizen but the same young guy is drawn to the flash of the mob guy...one day, the kid is walking down the street with Palminteri and one of the kid's friends crosses their path and De Niro's son starts chasing the other kid. Palminteri's character grabs him and asks why he's chasing the other to which the son says, "he owes me $10 bucks" to which Palminteri replies, "let him go for $10 dollars he's out of your life" (or something to that effect). The point here is this...you may pay a few people forward who never, ever respond...only take, take, take. You will quickly learn who they are if you're paying attention and then you can remove them from your life/network...there clearly is no connection there!

Let me give you a tool that many of you will (if you think this is valuable) do with a spreadsheet, but you can do with good old pencil, paper and ruler.

Lay the paper out in landscape mode and draw a grid...the left-hand margin should have enough room to write out someone's full name, the next margin wide enough for an email address, the next one for a telephone number...

From there, draw lines parallel to those you already drew but maybe half or a third of the width of the others.

Label the one furthest left NAME, the next one EMAIL, the next...you guessed it TELEPHONE (I'm going to suggest a cell phone would be best and will explain here in a moment).

Then label the rest of the columns with hobbies, food, places of interest, sports, books, movies, actors, musical artists, other artists, etc.

Write down the names of everybody you know in the name column and of course their corresponding contact info on those spaces...then, go across and put an "X" in each of the other boxes where you think content of some sort about that would interest that person...for me it might be songs, music movies, sports etc.

Then, while you're surfing the web or are on LinkedIn and see a piece that's intriguing, copy the link, search through your grid for others there who might appreciate it and send it to them...email, text whatever with a quick note, "Barry, long time no speak, hoping you're well. I saw this Springsteen article and it reminded me of you so I thought to share. Hoping to catch up soon! Love and kisses Bill."

Now, suppose you designated an hour a week or an hour a month or whatever to this "staying in touch, connecting" project...what do you think could happen when you possibly needed something that person may be able to help with? Would your chances be better, or worse that they might pay attention a bit more? If they don't, or cannot help, what have you lost?

Summing up the TRUTH about networking...

Stop, Look, LISTEN, connect in a genuine, authentic way and remain connected in the same fashion.

If you'd like a PDF version of the NETWORKING GRID I use in my classes and private consults...it's yours FREE for the asking.

Send an email to truth@barrykleiman.com and write Network Grid in SUBJECT Line

" Ba ba baba, baba ba baba, I wanna be sedated"

I Wanna Be Sedated

-The Ramones

CHAPTER 8

The Truth About Linkedin

I n the last Chapter, The TRUTH About Networking, we discussed the invaluable principle of listening. We also discussed that (for me anyway) the term "networking" itself is a misnomer...it really needs to be thought of as CONNECTING.

We also spoke of the fact that Networking/Connecting is a very viable mode of **MEDIA** to help you get your **MESSAGE** to your **MARKET**.

How the TRUTH Will Set You & Your Career Free - TRUTHS about LinkedIn

1. It too is yet another form of **MEDIA** to help one get their **MESSAGE** to **MARKET**.

2. Except for a few minor differences, the TRUTHS about LinkedIn are similar to the TRUTHS about cover letters...power exists in the use of both.

3. The TRUTH, with respect to LinkedIn alone, is that the power is potentially highly significant, however, there is also significant power in a chainsaw. If you know how to use it well, its value for getting any number of things accomplished is amazing...used improperly, it could cost you quite a lot.

4. LinkedIn, like your cover letter, should not to be used as just a replication of your resume.

5. LinkedIn may not always help, but it can rarely hurt, UNLESS you become very boring, sedating people by doing what everybody else does. *LinkedIn can really tie your entire background together and raise it to a prominence never before possible OR reduce you to a boring, ho-hum commodity.*

6. LinkedIn provides you the most active, widely viewed "billboard" the professional community has ever known. There are more than 450,000,000 members in over 200 countries. FOUR HUNDRED and FIFTY MILLION people can read everything you care to share about yourself, PLUS, you can post it for FREE!!!

Microsoft recently purchased LinkedIn for $26,200,000,000...that's BILLION with a "B" and did so of course *for many reasons I am sure...one of which is the opportunity to immediately access that installed base of professional users...*

*You can essentially have access to any number of those same people for a big fat **$0 Dollars.** (It's TRUE that there are paid versions of LinkedIn, and it's TRUE they may provide extra benefits, but I do not believe anyone should start their foray into using LinkedIn by paying).*

In Initial TRUTH #5 above, I mentioned a very important, "user beware" downside to this amazing MEDIA opportunity LinkedIn provides us all and that is this...

You do not want any of the 450,000,000 possible folks who can view your LinkedIn Profile to be sedated!!

"Marketing Sin #1 = Being Boring!!!"

Dan Kennedy

(Apologies, but here I go again...I guess I'm just a smitten storyteller!)

In the movie, **Ferris Bueller's Day Off,** there was a scene in an Economics class where the camera panned the classroom to show almost **every student asleep...some with drool dripping down their chin** as the teacher was pontificating...

"In 1930, the Republican-controlled House of Representatives, in an effort to alleviate the effects of the... Anyone? Anyone? ...the Great Depression, passed the... Anyone? Anyone? The tariff bill? The Hawley-Smoot Tariff Act? Which, anyone? Raised or lowered? ...raised tariffs, in an effort to collect more revenue for the federal government. Did it work? Anyone? Anyone know the effects? It did not work, and the United States sank deeper into the Great Depression. Today we have a similar debate over this. Anyone know what this is? Class? Anyone? Anyone? Anyone seen this before? The Laffer Curve. Anyone know what this says? It says that at this point on the revenue curve, you will get exactly the same amount of revenue as at this point. This is very controversial. Does anyone know what Vice President Bush called this in 1980? Anyone? Something-d-o-o economics. 'Voodoo' economics".

So... beside the fact that the scene itself is quite entertaining, I offer the above as a tangible example of a person bringing a boring **MESSAGE** to his **MARKET** via what TRULY is a **boring MEDIA.**

"How the TRUTH Will Set You & Your Career Free - SECRET

Your LinkedIn profile is quite possibly the greatest chance you'll ever have to tell your story to the world and back it up anecdotally. YOU DO NOT WANT TO HAVE IT TAKE ON THE SAME END RESULT AS FERRIS BUELLER'S ECON TEACHER!

Whether it occurs via your profile, what you yourself post, or the manner with which you respond to the posts of others, your opportunity to become more visible and potentially more viable has never been easier!

Imagine the enhancement to that visibility and viability with testimonials written about you by others (peers, superiors, neighbors, friends, civic leaders etc.).

Then imagine all of those testimonials carrying the same essential **MESSAGE** about you...things related to your expertise but also comments about your soft skill traits (otherwise difficult for anyone to quantify). You may not think things such as this are viable or valuable to which I'd say, "FINE...show me then some other tool that can help you become a more dimensional entity accessible to a scant 450,000,000 people."

The **MEDIA** that is LinkedIn can both help you promote your **MESSAGE** to the **MARKET** and even help you find/define a **MARKET**, but (and this is big!)...

If you're not ready to stand out with a **MESSAGE** that's interesting, unique, powerful, robust etc. STAY AWAY FROM LINKEDIN!

It's incredibly powerful...but so is a chainsaw!!

OK...hoping that helps you understand my mindset on LinkedIn overall. Think about it, if you're not yet convinced one way or the other, and are not yet sure that my logic makes sense, I suggest staying away or keeping your profile very, very simple...name, rank/serial number type of thing.

If what I had to say makes some sense and you'd like to proceed but you're just not quite sure how, please do read on...what follows should help you create a powerful LinkedIn profile (aka **MESSAGE**).

How the TRUTH Will Set You & Your Career Free - SECRET

Facts tell but stories sell!

While I'm not going to get into defending this cutesy little rhyme/quote too much, I will recommend a few things to read that should help corroborate the comment.

Consider reading:

- **Winning the Story Wars**: Why Those Who Tell - and Live - the Best Stories Will Rule the Future by Jonah Sachs

- **The Power of Story** by Jim Loeher

- Double Your Income in 6 Months Using LinkedIn - Joe Bartling (This is a personal favorite of mine and though now written more than a decade ago, it still is amazing AND IT'S FREE!) Here's a link: http://www.spiderware.com/linkedin/Double_Your_Income_in_6_Months_Using_LinkedIn.pdf

To be clear:

A certain number of facts need to be included in your LinkedIn profile.

You must do all that you can to insure those facts are easily accessible early on...best foot forward type of thing (titles, dates, relevant industry specifics etc.).

You want to do this by telling a story about it all as here's a chance, in front of 450,000,000 people to share "the uniqueness of you".

Read the Joe Bartling piece...you'll get some sense of what I mean...it's been the guiding light of my own profile for quite some time now!

Can I give you a couple of tools?

One you can use to make telling your story a bit easier and another to grade yourself on your efforts.

"How the TRUTH Will Set You & Your Career Free" - SECRET Story Building Tool:

Go back to the index cards you wrote out as you were building your MESSAGE.

Having a *consistent authenticity* is vital anyway, so let's use some of the things you wrote earlier about the value you bring along with its benefit to the end user and begin to craft a story behind each of those values and benefits.

Craft each story with "soft skills" you had to use to get that job done effectively.

Did you need to buy pizza for the group?

Did you have to stay late 9 nights in a row, get giddy, fall asleep during segments of the process, eat the same meals each night, bet the group by what date the project would be finished?

What was your greatest take-away?

What did you learn about yourself that you've carried forward since?

There are a ton of other questions you could ask and answer to allow you to be you to the reader, but that provides them with a dimension about you that they wouldn't otherwise know.

Facts tell but stories sell!

"How the TRUTH Will Set You & Your Career Free" - SECRET Profile Grading Tool:

I call this The LinkedIn Litmus Test.

You may find this quick test initially humbling but it will prove invaluable if taken to heart!

Type the title of **your most recent job** into the SEARCH BAR on LinkedIn and hit ENTER.

If you're considering employment in another field or with a title/functional area of responsibility other than is currently on your resume, type that instead and hit ENTER.

How many other of the 450,000,000 LinkedIn folks have similar titles?

Compare your profile to theirs.

Why would someone pick you and not them or vice versa?

"It is not worth an intelligent man's time to be in the majority. By definition, there are already enough people to do that."

Godfrey Harold Hardy, English Mathematician

The idea is to stand out not blend in.

The statistical majority is always wrong.

If you do what everybody else does, you get what everybody else gets.

Dare to be you.

Allow people to know you.

Not everybody will like you any more than everybody likes chocolate cake; I for one hate butterscotch but plenty of it sells!

Be honest always with your market...practice operating with *consistent authenticity* as your brand.

"How the TRUTH Will Set You & Your Career Free" - SECRET

If you're genuinely interested in standing out (as opposed to blending in), let me strongly suggest you study the work of a great copywriter or two.

(A copywriter is a person who writes the text for advertising or promotional material)

If you don't have much interest in the science of how the power of words can leverage the power of your knowledge, that's your choice...

Before you make that choice let me at least share with you that coming to understand and apply a bit of a copywriter's knowledge is one of the single greatest, highly leverage-able, under-taught skills in our educational system today.

Once again, science is involved.

You're ultimately dealing with people who are by nature complicated.

Remember...you cannot solve complex problems with simple solutions so not taking into account, learning then applying a few principles of copywriting is done at your own risk of blending in!

If you have the interest but cannot find the time to get into the skill too deeply, I can provide you the formula I most use with my clients. There are many for sure though I more often than not default to this alliterative three word lesson...

Benefits, Believability, Bounce:

Remember the words of Mark Joyner's The Irresistible Offer.

When you write or speak about anything you'd like someone to consider on a level beyond just the sound of your voice, make 100% certain to include in your **MESSAGE...**

BENEFITS, BELIEVABILITY and BOUNCE...otherwise you risk having the same reaction taken on by Ferris Bueller's classmates!

Summing this all up and keeping CORE CONCEPT #1 in mind...

You are a "Marketeer".

In order for people to consider what it is you're **MARKETING**, you must make them well aware of what you do and what you've done, and want to put it in a story form.

You want to present your expertise up-front.

You want to tell people how they would **benefit** by being involved with somebody like yourself.

You want to tell them in a story at some level that includes not just the **benefit**, but (anecdotally with your story) why they should **believe** you, and ultimately, the **benefit** they will derive from working with you.

You want to be able to tell them who you are aside from a business professional, (Unless that's all you care about, though I'd say watch out if that's all that you want out of your work!).

LinkedIn is a very powerful tool that needs to be understood as such...remembering the chainsaw analogy along the way...use it but use it wisely.

If you're interested in signing up for one of our regularly scheduled The TRUTH About How to be LinkedIn webinars let me know via email to: truth@barrykleiman.com and write Webinar in the SUBJECT.

CHAPTER 9

The Truth About Cover Letters

W hat's needed for the construction of a TRULY effective COVER LETTER including the mindset is discussed in large part in Chapter 8, The TRUTH About LinkedIn.

In my way of thinking, the purposes of your LinkedIn profile and your Cover Letter are near identical. I'll do my very best here to explain the differences...some are quite subtle, though principally speaking, their purposes are the same.

There is one main difference to me; you can have a different cover letter for different jobs; your LinkedIn profile should do more about describing YOU than a specific role...your skills, your traits, your story (and hopefully a bunch of TESTIOMINALS validating it all).

One of the most hotly discussed topics on the Internet these days (related to Cover Letters) is "Do I actually really need one? Isn't it just repeating my resume?"

The simple TRUTH is you may or may not NEED a cover letter! As for it being a replication of your resume, I'd say that would be a big mistake.

Cover letters may not always help, though rarely do they hurt...unless of course you break Marketing Sin #1 (Don't Be Boring) and that would be the case if yours is simply replicating your resume.

We already discussed How the TRUTH Will Set You & Your Career Free - SECRET "Facts Tell But Stories Sell".

I'll add to that a bit here with another seemingly cutesy saying that is a well-known parable amongst all great marketers ...

"The more you tell, the more you sell".

Upcoming in Chapter 10 - The TRUTH About Resumes, where we discuss in detail the key specific TRUTHS about that document. The essence of it all though resumes is this; they are a collection of facts and in almost all cases initially get a 6 second look...6 seconds!

You TRULY need to not only know this but also accept it as fact when you pen yours. There are other considerations such as "keywords" etc. which we will discuss further in the next chapter, but for all intents and purposes...the six second rule is in effect with your resume!

Now...if you're good enough, if you're clever enough, if you study the art of writing enough, your cover letter can be the story that sells the rest of you. This point will certainly be argued by many people saying: "I never look at cover letters" and that may very well be, THOUGH...I contend the opposite!

I also strongly contend that someone who doesn't want to know more about you than the facts attached to your resume is looking at you through what I call a "commodity lens". They are looking at you with a "soybean", "pork belly" type of mindset whereas I believe more in the "uniqueness of you" (which we discussed earlier).

*My contention about not needing or someone saying they never look at a cover letter also stems from the fact that a job search marketing campaign that does not include a cover letter is missing a **MEDIA** opportunity to bring your **MESSAGE** to your **MARKET**.*

Imagine someone committed to filling a key role in their organization trying to decide between one resume or another...

Would it be impossible for you then to imagine the impact of a well thought out, well-reasoned, well formatted cover letter with a captivating/fascinating story, and what impact it might have on the person doing the hiring?

Can you imagine a scenario where that well thought out, well-reasoned, well formatted cover letter with a captivating/fascinating story would do more harm than good?

Even a very brief story can go a really long way in breaking ties between any two people that may be in the mind of the potential interviewer. Your cover letter can take the facts and tie it together with who you are as a person, as a human being, and as a personality.

In the last chapter, we spoke of learning the skill of a copywriter and using the classic **Benefit, Believability, Bounce** formula. Its goal is simply teaching you how to grab attention and how to keep somebody reading and interested. In our seminar, webinars and private consultations, we teach it on a far deeper level than can be provided here, but please think about how you might use those **Three Bs** as you consider sharing the "uniqueness of you" in print.

Below are questions I get asked most often about **Cover Letters** that you may have too:

- "What's the best format for the cover letter?"

- "How do I keep people interested?"

If you give any credence to the "facts tell but stories sell' secret, you'd give credence to this...

If you tell a story, if you tell your story, if you find a way to engage people and teach them the "uniqueness of you", they'll get more attached to you.

The format for this "story" could be of any kind.

There could be a picture of a concept or point you're trying to make, with surrounding quotes illuminating your most defining principles.

There could be a "grabber", the purpose of which would be the same as the picture noted above.

(A "grabber" is a three dimensional thing an example of which could be as simple as a penny attached to your cover letter in a hand-addressed, snail-mailed" envelope).

There could be a flow chart.

When's the last time you saw a resume or a cover letter that had a flow chart (laying out your problem-solving thought process or something of the kind) instead of a traditional cover letter?

Once again, you are a "Marketeer". You want to display your value. You have to be creative enough to find a way to do it, otherwise you won't. You'll blend in. Don't blend in if you expect to stand out.

- What's the best length for my cover letter?"

I don't think a cover letter should even be a full page but it could be.

Remember though, once again Marketing Sin #1 - DO NOT BE BORING. You must not have anyone interpret what you're saying or what you're doing as *"blah, blah, blah"*.

A great guidepost as to whether or not you're on the *"blah, blah, blah"* track is when you write something, whether a paragraph or a whole cover letter, ask yourself this simple question: "So what?" If what you're trying to say doesn't pass that simple test...if it's not interesting and valuable, re-do it or leave it out!!!

(Once again), the real purpose of a cover letter once again is providing color commentary to your background. It flavors it. It allows people to get to know you behind the facts that are on your resume (dates, schools, job titles career progression etc.).

It's a little bit more you.

Your friend may think a cover letter is a bad idea...I'm here to tell you they are almost never bad ideas, **unless they're boring**.

- "What do you write about?"

You write about the TRUTH!

Your cover letter is an amazing opportunity to take yourself from commodity/porkbelly status, to status of "interesting", "intriguing", "authentic" you may ever have **with someone you've never met**.

If you've been downsized - TELL THE TRUTH.

If you've been the victim of an even dicier situation - TELL THE TRUTH.

If you have a felony on your record - TELL THE TRUTH.

Can you imagine the tremendous "not-blend-in" opportunity possible by starting your cover letter with a big picture of a STOP SIGN at the top and underneath write something such as:

STOP!!!

"I am a convicted felon."

"I wanted you to know that before you read any further".

"If by virtue of that fact you wouldn't consider hiring me, I've saved us both a lot of time by letting you know that upfront."

"My skills and expertise in the areas of X Y Z could add great value to the problems related to WHATEVER POSITION YOU'RE APPLYING FOR, but I understand if an issue from 7 years ago would preclude you hiring me today".

Many, many people will try to tell you "Try to keep it covered up."...I think that's as bad an idea as you could possibly imagine.

Again, a cover letter is a chance to tell your story. If you're good at it, you can overcome some of the things that other people try to sweep under the carpet. On your resume, I say put your best foot up front. On your cover letter, if there is something that's really bad or you're embarrassed about or think could hurt you, I would tell you to put right near the top of your cover letter.

Tell the TRUTH and tell it straight away...you'll be amazed by its impact!

I'll close this chapter with a brief example of how your cover letter is both a form of **MEDIA** to get your **MESSAGE** to the **MARKET** as well as a potential lead generator...

"How the TRUTH Will Set You & Your Career Free" - SECRET

Share your cover letter with somebody you know. This person may or may not know you're looking for a new role, however, if you ask them their opinion you can get both insight as well as inform them about what's happening in your life.

Start with a disclaimer something like the following...

Dear Jim,

Thanks in advance for taking the time to read what I wrote below and offering your opinion...it really shouldn't take you more than 90-100 seconds to read, but would mean a great deal to me!

You should know that I came to this format after reading a book by this maniacal guy who thought I should tell the TRUTH all of the time including here on my cover letter. Please be honest with me as I value your opinion greatly.

You're obviously never going to get a hundred percent buy in from everybody.

They make chocolate and vanilla flavors of ice cream for a reason, however, worst case scenario, you are giving somebody a chance to hear your story that they may otherwise not have had a chance to hear...and with your brand of the **TRUTH** evident everywhere.

Consistent authenticity has exponential impact!

The **TRUTH** is a brand.

The **TRUTH** is a strategy.

The **TRUTH** is a mindset that will supersede all others if you allow it.

If your brand, strategy or mindset is not the **TRUTH**, then what is in its place?

Cover letters may not always help but they can rarely hurt and often provide great leverage...ensuring you're not viewed through a "commodity lens".

No "EIEIO" for you!

OK...up next The TRUTH About Your Resume...the part that most people are waiting to hear. (Were you able to take on the challenge and not read Chapter 10 until now?)

It's Chapter 10 not because it's not important...clearly it is! Let's discuss WHY and HOW to optimize its place in the "How the TRUTH Will Set You & Your Career Free" process.

"I'm sick and tired of hearing things
From uptight, short-sighted, narrow-minded hypocritics
All I want is the truth
Just gimme some truth"

Gimme Some Truth

-John Lennon

CHAPTER 10

The Truth About Resumes

Well, we've finally come to the point in this book that you may find even more contentious than some of what preceded this chapter.

I spent as much time thinking through the quote above from John Lennon as I did any other part of what's written, simply because in my way of thinking, not only is this the TRUTH but I am also sick and tired of hearing things to the contrary.

Of course, your resume is an important piece of the equation, HOWEVER...

What I do need to make 100% clear is my position on the fact that it's just that, A PIECE of the equation no more...no less.

Like any piece of any puzzle though, it must fit in to the proper place. If you calibrate its impact in any other way, you will be (as another song goes) "looking for love in all the wrong places".

I'm going to use a transcription from another seminar I taught for the bulk of this chapter, only because the questions asked then seem to be asked again and again and again.

Before I do that, allow me to provide a few overarching comments that could save you a quite a bit of time...

"How the TRUTH Will Set You & Your Career Free" - SECRET

I believe, have observed, as well as have been party to the fact that...

Resumes are first judged as art!

What that means is this:

Far, far more often than not, your resume first needs to be appealing to the eye. Will it be easy to look at/read?

If someone picks up a resume with small fonts, tight spacing, funny formatting or anything else that precludes the reader from finding the information they most need to know QUICKLY, that resume will be dismissed...not read!

Now, you may choose not to believe that or you may think that's the case for other resumes but not yours, so I will share with you this other fact "denial is not a river in Egypt".

Let me back this empirically based opinion with some harder data…

Type into Google "How long does a hiring manager look at a resume?" or some similar iteration of this question.

The answer? 6 seconds…6 seconds!

I mentioned this in the last chapter and am doing so again now as it cannot be stressed enough.

You operating with the thought that the resume is the epicenter of the entire job search is what's been taught by multitudes of people in seeming positions of authority/power simply because that's what they know…that's what they've been taught.

If what's on your resume is all that you have as your MESSAGE to MARKET, then all you have is your resume.

If all you have is your resume as the MEDIA to deliver you MESSAGE to MARKET, then all you have is your resume.

Your entire marketing campaign is based on 6 seconds of maybe!

Is that really what you think of yourself and of the value you provide?

If that's the case, well then I wish you great success in your life and your career...I wish you and your family health and prosperity. Personally though, I'd never leave my career success, job search sanity and life's prosperity to a wish.

If you're trying to honor yourself, your life, your career, your family and are betting all of that with 6 seconds as your leverage...I'd strongly suggest you read this book again!

(Also, maybe buy a few lottery tickets and wish you'd win when you do ☺)

Here is the Q&A from a recent seminar

Speaker:

What's the best format? Is it chronological or functional?

Barry:

Actually, it's not necessarily either.

The main thing with a resume is to get your best foot forward and do so very, very quickly because, in my experience and opinion, having read literally a hundred-thousand or more resumes, resumes are first judged as art, which basically means if somebody looks at it first and it's too cramped or the font or color is bad, they won't look at it again.

With even that said, it's been proven that a resume gets about 6 seconds. I'd worry less about format and more about getting your best foot forward.

Speaker:

All right. Do I need a picture?

Barry:

Beauty is in the eye of the beholder, but I would say, absolutely not.

Speaker:

How many pages do I need?

Barry:

I'm going to go back to my comment earlier. Resumes get 6 seconds, so however many pages you think will take a reader 6 seconds, is how many pages you should have.

What I am trying to say is do your very, very best to get it on 1 page and get your best foot forward right at the top.

Speaker:

How important are employment dates?

Barry:

Sorry, call me "Broken Record Barry", I'm going to answer the question as I did before. Get your best foot forward.

What you don't want to happen on your resume, is for it to be a treasure hunt. If your dates are important, if you have good stability in your work, absolutely put your dates on there. Connect the dots for people right away. Your resume is also not a trash dump. You don't want to just start piling on word after word after word, hoping you'll snow somebody. Make the dates available if they add value and if they don't add value, don't put them on.

Speaker:

Okay. what about using certain keywords? Are there any I must use?

Barry:

Probably...

TRUTH be told I am hardly an expert in this subject but am certain there are many books/blog posts written on that subject.

My instinct is that if a job description asks for certain skills those skills should be included (as keywords) on your resume

Here again...I go back to an earlier comment about having a multi-tiered, multi-faceted modes of MEDIA to get your MESSAGE to the MARKET...your resume is one for sure...I just believe deeply that you need more! I do not think any of our lives, career success or job search sanity should be dependent solely on guessing the correct keywords.

Speaker:

Okay.

Barry

I hate to keep saying this, but believe it's the most important thing you'll ever know about a resume. You get 6 seconds!

There's an old TV show called Dragnet where the Sergeant Friday said, "Just give me the facts, ma'am, just the facts." I wouldn't worry as much about keywords. I'd worry about getting my best foot forward.

Speaker:

Are there words I should avoid?

Barry:

Probably...whereas you may be able to do so in the correct context of your cover letter I'd stay away from any kind of cutesy, colloquial terms on your resume. I'd stay away from anything that just will make you seem unprofessional. Certainly no curse words, I think is the best way to go about it. Other than that, no, again, you're trying to get someone to understand the facts.

Speaker:

What does not belong on a resume?

Barry:

Everything on your resume should be relevant to your career or your character.

I would avoid politics.

I would avoid religion.

I would avoid sexual preference and keep it to things that are relevant to, again, your career or your character.

I would avoid salary information unless of course it's specifically requested...this is almost never a way for it to go well for you the job seeker

Community things are fine. Things you've done for your community are fine, but avoid controversial issues, like politics, religion, sexual preferences.

Speaker:

Thank you...seems like very good advice.

So, there you have it...

As I've said hundreds and hundreds of times in my career, "a resume by itself almost never got anyone a job, but it has precluded many from getting one".

Its function in your **MARKETING** is that of both **MESSAGE** and **MEDIA** and it only gets SIX SECONDS to do both...get your best foot forward and pronto!

Its goal is a simple one...evoke enough curiosity in the reader to induce a next step in the form of an interview.

Speaking of an interview...the chapter on The TRUTH About Interviewing is on the next page.

> *Overture, curtains, lights,*
> *This is it, the night of nights*
> *No more rehearsing and nursing a part*
> *We know every part by heart*
> *Overture, curtains, lights*
> *This is it, you'll hit the heights*
> *And oh what heights we'll hit*
> *On with the show this is it"*
>
> The Bugs Bunny Theme

CHAPTER 11

The Truth About Interviews
Showtime!

I n our last chapter, we discussed the TRUTH about RESUMES...

How they are first judged as art... their construction, their purpose and the inconvenient TRUTH that regardless of what you write, your resume gets a 6 second look! (10 if you're really, really lucky!)

We also discussed how they act in a dual role of your **MARKETING** campaign, **MESSAGE** and **MEDIA.**

(This is important for two reasons, as they can help you twice or hurt you twice)

This chapter, "**The Truth About Interviewing**" has a subtitle of, "**Showtime!**" and here's why...

You've done enough of the right things to this point in your campaign to actually have an interview. Congratulations!

It's now **SHOWTIME!**

It's now time for you to walk the walk and talk the talk!

I want to delve deeply into the opportunity in front of you, but before I do, I'd like to share yet another...

"How the TRUTH Will Set You & Your Career Free - SECRET

You're almost always interviewing!

I've already shared with you the story I know first-hand about the client of mine sitting in a Starbucks in Sunnyvale, California and accidently had hot coffee dropped in his lap, on his new suit by the CEO of a large local multi-billion-dollar company. Instead of reacting like the person on the subway did, he was very gracious, and how he wound up working for the CEO...but I have an even better...at least maybe more amusing example described below beginning with a tweet called KARMA...

TWEET:

Karma – the guy who pushed past me on the tube then suggested I go F myself just arrived for his interview...with me...

STORY:

In February 2015, Matt Buckland tweeted an encounter that goes down in viral history as one of the best examples of instant karma.

On his way to work during Monday morning rush hour in London, Matt was standing on the Tube when a man pushed past him nearly knocking him over.

As if that wasn't bad enough the man, in a rush, began swearing at him.

Not a great way to start the workweek but Matt continued on with his day at Forward Partners, where he works as the head of talent and recruiting. When five o'clock came around, he prepared for his interview with a potential new hire.

When his interviewee showed up to the office Matt couldn't help but recognize the man standing before him, resume in hand...

As you might imagine the "interviewee" in this story did not get the job but you must admit it's a pretty darn good example of my "You're almost always interviewing" premise.

The truth is, that as you read this book, I'm being interviewed by you!

You're trying to decide if you think I know what the heck I'm talking about...if my comments and commentary make any sense at all. Maybe they do, maybe they don't. You have to decide that. I'm in an interview right now, trying to add value to you and to your understanding of this process.

I believe you're always interviewing.

You want to be the same person all the time.

Consistent authenticity resonates everywhere you go and that's an over-arching theme to everything we do.

SHOWTIME is all of the time, but let's discuss the rest of the TRUTH about Interviewing!

Have you ever gone into an interview uncertain about the overall process of interviewing itself?

> Or maybe you were just uncertain about whether or not the specific opportunity for which were interviewing fit your specific career goals?

> Or maybe you were clear about those things but uncertain about the culture of the company?

> Or maybe you knew all of those things but were uncertain about how to best explain your strengths, or,

best explain or answer that "weakness" question that we all know and dread.

We actually teach an entire course on this one topic, but for now, I'll do my very best to encapsulate it all here.

If you're truly honest with yourself and answered yes to even one of the preceding questions or those questions emoted any level of anxiety for an upcoming interview, you are not alone for sure, so here's some really good news...

I believe that all the work you've done to this point, the **MESSAGES** you've created along with the TRUTHS you've surrounded yourself with will help you develop a systematic approach to all of your interviewing.

Remember, what we've been working on is a system...a process rooted in your TRUTHS affording you the freedom of little doubt...you just need to TRUST yourself. If you've done the work, the rest will be "easier".

Interviewing is interviewing is interviewing is interviewing.

Whether you're 15 or 50, or 25 or 65, that's the case. You're sitting there, trying to convey the value of what you do to the person or people asking the questions and...

You're trying your best to do so in a manner that's conversant as opposed to robotic.

"How the TRUTH Will Set You & Your Career Free" - NUGGET:

The best interviews are conversations not interrogations.

To say "interviewing is interviewing is interviewing" might leave someone to think that all interviews are the same and they are decidedly not. All one needs to do is read a column in the Sunday New York Times called **The Corner Office** to make that clear.

I recommend reading the Corner Office as much as possible as it will anecdotally put on full display that all interviews are not alike. Each week, the columnist interviews the CEO from companies all across business spectrums, and each week one of the topics discussed are their hiring practices/interview methodologies.

Reading it will provide great proof as to why I loathe the blogs posts and articles highlighting the "10 Best Interview Questions" or the "3 Answers You Must Be Prepared to Use During Your Interview" etc. (What will often be made clear is the fact that what you read in the last chapter about resumes is far more than opinion).

Your job as an interviewee, however, is always the same. You have to have a **MESSAGE** that conveys the value that you bring to the person or the people on the other side of the desk. Being prepared to do this is mission critical and what we've been working toward to this point.

Interviewing can really be difficult and there's definitely not any one single 100% fool-proof method except to:

- Understand and know your TRUTHS

- LISTEN carefully so you know exactly what type of information is being sought

- Explain in an anecdotal, example-laden way your TRUTHS as they relate to the question(s)...

There are many types of interviews. There are informational interviews, there are exploratory interviews, there's standard job search interviews and each of those have separate components:

- Telephone interviews,

- Skype interviews,

- email interviews,

- (Of course) traditional, face-to-face interviews and those that have yet another subset of potential iterations such as one on one or "gauntlet" style interviews.

- There are behavior type of interviews, with questions about things like your biggest failure

- There are situational interviews. "What would you do if...?"

- There are case study interviews

- There are presentation interviews whereby you need to present a solution to a problem in a short period of time.

- There are "stress" interviews

Here's a quick, simple exercise that, once done, will provide great dividends to any interview you'll ever have (and it's a great use of your resume too!).

Despite the fact that your resume is viewed with the "6 second rule", initially, by the time an interview takes place any number of questions are induced from things on that document.

Whether it's just dates or schools or hobbies or whatever, often times, your resume serves as a guide for the person on the other side of the desk.

(Even if that's not always the case, this exercise will prove incredibly worthwhile)

Go grab another stack of index cards like you used to create your **MESSAGE**.

Use one card for EVERY LINE ITEM on your resume:

On the front of each card, write down the item you're referencing, then, on the back of the card, write out bullet points that will help you tell a story about that item. If you cannot think of a story, then write a metaphor, or a movie line or song lyric...something that will remind you of how to best explain whatever it is you're referencing.

How The Truth Will Set You & Your Career Free

(In case you can't tell, I use lyrics all of the time)

PLEASE DO THIS!

You will be doing yourself a tremendous favor if you do.

Even the Rolling Stones rehearse...you can/should/need to rehearse, too.

Professionals practice, amateurs hope!

You only get one chance to make a first impression...be prepared!

Don't assume you'll remember...

Prepare! Make as certain as certain can be that you understand yourself and how you would best explain every part, every nuance, every component of your history.

Please understand that you TRULY have no clue what's going to come your way once an interview begins.

There are some interviews I've been involved with where the interviewer literally sat with his back to the candidate and threw a softball up against the wall.

There have been interviews where people only ask one question such as "Tell me the worst thing that happened in your childhood".

There are interviews of every kind and you need to be able to discuss things as fluidly and TRUTHFULLY as possible.

This includes being able to say: "I don't know" OR "I've not done that before; I can tell you how I've dealt previously with other situations when confronted with things I've never done before, but if you're asking about that skill in particular, I TRULY have no experience"

Here's the deal...unless what's being asked is inappropriate (things like religion or politics etc.)...you're there to answer questions.

You want to tell the TRUTH!

I mentioned this earlier but in case you're skimming...

If you're a convicted felon, tell the TRUTH!

If you were fired from your last job or placed on academic probation (like I once was), tell the TRUTH!

If you were once placed on disciplinary probation (like I once was), tell the TRUTH!

If you walk into an interview and somebody says, "Well, tell me the thing you'd like me to least know about you" tell them the TRUTH (then of course, with stories, and tangible examples, explain what's transpired since in your life...highlighting it all with your "value add").

I'll keep repeating this as it's the essence of everything else I believe and have written...

The TRUTH is a BRAND.

The TRUTH is a STRATEGY.

The TRUTH is a MINDSET that kicks the crap out of any other.

Because I do believe that the best interviews are conversations not interrogations and because I don't think you should have "scripted" questions, I want to share with you a template for the five things that you, the interviewee, should be covering in an interview given the time to ask questions.

"How the TRUTH Will Set You & Your Career Free" - SECRET

Questions convey values!

- *When purchasing a home, parents with young kids almost always inquire about the schools in the neighborhood*

- *People who care about their carbon footprint ask questions about emissions from autos as they shop for cars. (People who drive Hummers do not...they ask about towing capacity etc.)*

Please understand that either implicitly or explicitly, the questions you ask show a great deal about what you deem important, so...

While I do not want you to interpret the following as "scripts" I would tell you that as topics they will not only provide you with an enormous amount of information, it will also be information not otherwise attainable without their use. There are ancillary benefits to using these topics/talking points (or some reasonable facsimile), which is providing the interviewer a sense of who you are on a level including but exceeding your knowledge on a particular topic. This is a good thing!

You may find the following somewhat controversial...you may not find it in other books, though I assure you it will be very centering. It will also provide an additional benefit of being able to conduct a conversation that has the capacity to scale...you'll be able to use the essential same template inside the same company again and again and, to a great end.

I share this very powerful collection of topics with everybody I've associated with during the past decades...my own family included.

Question Topic #1

Learn about the other person!

If you have time to ask one question and one question only to the interviewer, I would say, "Would you mind telling me something about yourself?"

It is beyond my imagination and instinct that there's anything more important than to know about the person with whom you're meeting.

If their reply is something like: "Well, what would you like to know?"

My comment would be, "Anything you would like to tell me."

(e.g. "Is that a picture of your dog behind you?" OR "Did you get a hole in one" "Whatever it is you'd like to share, I'd be interested in knowing")

Remember, the best interviews are conversations not interrogations...

You want to have dialogue and people ultimately like to talk about themselves.

If the person doesn't want to talk about himself or herself...if they tell you it's none of your business, that would be a big red flag for me! You could be working with this person for the rest of your life.

My thought process here is aimed at you just making as sure as you can that having a functional relationship with that person is possible.

Question Topic #2 and **#2A**

Understanding every nuance of the job **from that person's perspective**.

Whether or not the job has already been described, you must not be at all reluctant to dig deeper for the purpose of optimizing your understanding the role. If there were things you either didn't understand or simply needed to know for greater clarity...ASK.

DO NOT BE AFRAID THIS WILL SHED YOU IN A BAD LIGHT.

You have every right to know why the position is open (replacement, new hire etc).

You have every right to know everything it is you might be doing in the coming weeks/months/years.

The "right" organization will respect your attention to and appreciation of detail.

(#2A) In this same vein of quantifying the role, you also want to take the time to "right any wrong".

e.g. If you tripped over a question...

If you were asked the answer to 2 + 2 and you said 8, this would be a good time to say, "Well, this is not so much a question, Mr. Interviewer, but a while back you asked me about 2 + 2 and I screamed 8 because I thought you were going to ask me about 2 cubed. I wouldn't be able to sleep tonight if I didn't walk out of here correcting myself." We all know the answer's 4, you may as well let him/her know you're well aware the answer is 4.

Don't worry about correcting yourself seeming like a negative...in fact, it's just the opposite...it shows character...it shows intellect. Make sure you understand the job and every nuance of it.

I mentioned this template of topics being "scaleable", here's an example of just how that might work...

Let's say you wind up meeting four other people in the company during the interview process and use these same topics/questions; you may find out that Person A has a different interpretation of the job than Person B who has a different interpretation than Person C and so forth.

Major problem!!

You will never succeed in a job where four different people have four different sets of expectations. Make sure, when you have an opportunity to talk to EACH person that you understand the job from HIS OR HER perspective.

Question Topic #3

Defining/understanding success

"What does success look like in this job? Who are our internal customers and what do we need to do to keep them happy?" It's an offshoot of **Question Topic #2**, so you need to know that expectations are aligned. If each person in the decision chain thinks the customers are different and what keeps them happy are different, it's going to be a tough job!

Question Topic #4

Company culture

YOU: "What's it like to work here?"

THEM: "What does that mean?"

YOU: "You mentioned a few moments ago (like maybe when you asked that same person to "tell you about themselves") that you've been here for 6 years. How, if at all has the culture evolved?"

OR

"You mentioned you've been here less than a year. What's it like to work here vs. your previous company?"

Every company has a culture...do everything you can to understand this one from that person's perspective. It is a complete "Win-Win" to do so.

If you're asked why you want to know, you can simply/TRUTHFULLY state something to the effect of:

"If I am fortunate enough to get a job offer, I would really like to have all the information I possibly can to make the best decision for all of us concerned."

Anybody who doesn't want you to know this information or anybody who thinks it's none of your business is a person you do not want to work for...this I can assure you of with a high degree of confidence.

Last, but not least, Question Topic #5

The Future

Given the time, I'd certainly encourage you to discuss the future in a format similar to the following...

"Mrs. Interviewer, if I came to work here and did this job in a fashion that made you very happy...if I did ABC and XYZ, and did

so with the parameters we discussed in mind...what types of opportunities could a position like this lead to TWO YEARS DOWN THE ROAD?"

(If you cited specific examples that you learned along the way of the earlier parts of the interview that would be a GREAT way to do this!)

What all of this is doing is showing that you care about your future, while at the same time, showing that you really understand that it's going to take time to prove yourself. You're also showing that you understand the job as they explained it to you.

There's nothing wrong with wanting to do more and know more and have a promotion opportunity. **It would not be the first thing you would ask!**

The **Question Topics** I just laid out for you are very sequential.

1. You're going to find out first about the person you're meeting with,

2. Their interpretation of the job,

3. Their interpretation of the customers (internal and/or external) and what success looks like to them,

4. Their interpretation of the culture,

5. Their interpretation of the future.

It would be a bad idea to walk in and say, "Nice to meet you, Mrs. So-and-So. When do I get promoted?"

We should talk about things like **how to dress on an interview**.

While this comment may also be met with some degree of controversy I would always say conservatively...no less than "business casual". In today's market and here in Silicon Valley, people don't always wear ties or sports jackets to interviews. Though I contend I still would opt in that direction (or corresponding attire for women). If, when you walk in the door you notice some attire related disconnect and you feel uncomfortable, mention it! While anything is possible I cannot imagine a circumstance where saying something about not being clear on specific dressing choices but wanting to be as presentable as possible could be of any harm at all. Again, have a conversation. Be a human being. Be TRUTHFUL.

Don't be afraid to tell the TRUTH in interviews and everywhere else...in fact, **be afraid not to**!

Always just explain why you're making the comment or asking the questions you are but be TRUTHFUL. Somebody may not like it, that's for sure, but the reality is, somebody may not like a lie you tell.

If you are clear, if you're concise, if you give reasons WHY, that's your best chance to scale. If you walk in from a single interview, (get past round one) and you get into some of the more prominent, gauntlet-style interviews that are around today, (you know the kind...like when you're in a room with five or so people), you'd better have the TRUTH. *"Consistent authenticity* as well as the supporting stories!

Otherwise...one glitch and you're done!

This all started with you writing your W.I.N Statement.

You understood what was important, now stick to it.

If you can't trust yourself, then who can you trust?

Remember...this is your challenge to become you!

It's your life, it's your time, it's your career.

Living a lie is just a horrible, horrible way to be. Understand the TRUTH and understand how it's best explained.

Coming up...the Follow Up

(That's where the fortune is...)

If you're interested in signing up for one of our regularly scheduled The TRUTH About Interviewing webinars let me know by sending an email to:

truth@barrykleiman.com and write Truth Webinar in the SUBJECT.

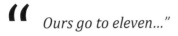 *Ours go to eleven..."*

This is Spinal Tap
Nigel Tufnel

CHAPTER 12

The Truth About The Follow-Up

We talked about interviewing, and now your interview is over. Hopefully, you were able to cover in specific, tangible, anecdotal story-type format, YOUR story...YOUR TRUTHS.

Hopefully, you were interesting.

Hopefully, you were dynamic.

Hopefully, you were not boring! Boring is a sin.

If so, you did a great job. Your verbal marketing pitch was great.

With your opportunity to get in front of your audience and see how compelling you can be, you were amazing.

As a "Marketeer" though, you have one more big job.

Any "Marketeer" worth their salt will tell you "the fortune is in the follow-up", and you are now in the follow-up stage.

Hopefully, you got the card of the person you were meeting.

If you didn't, it's easy enough to find out where they are, get a mailing address, and so forth.

Now, how do you follow-up?

We've talked about this from the early on days and we now find ourselves circling back at the **MESSAGE, MARKET, MEDIA** model.

You know who your **MARKET** is at this point, it's now incumbent on you to craft the appropriate follow-up **MESSAGE** then use the correct **MEDIA** to get it there safely.

(For my way of thinking) the **MESSAGE** is threefold:

1. How appreciative you are for the time they spent interviewing you.

2. How interested you are in the job, **and for what reasons**. 2 (A) *If you felt as though you blew an answer how much you kicked yourself for not providing a clear enough response to XYZ.*

3. How you look forward to hearing back from them, and that they should reach out to you if they have any questions, comments or concerns.

You'll also want to be 100% certain you include all of your contact information!

Home Phone, Mobile Phone, EMAIL Address etc.

I'm going to recommend you approach this follow-up in two ways,

Snail Mail and email...and, I'm going to recommend that if at all possible you follow-up both ways with a bonus...a grabber, as it were.

Often in interviews, stories or book or PDFs or some type of examples have been referenced. (Based on everything that has been written thus far I would hope that you have used some of these during your interview).

It is not beyond my belief, nor should it be beyond your belief, that it'd be worth your investment in a book or a printed copy of a PDF, or a soft copy of the PDF in your email, in your "snail mail" or both, when you follow-up. (This of course is all depending on your level of interest)

Something like this could work...

P.S. "By the way, Barry, here's a copy of that book we discussed. Regardless of your interest, or how this all turns out,

I think you'll enjoy it and I think it'll be valuable to you on a number of levels.

Thanks once again for taking the time to meet".

The question often comes to me about how often should one "follow up" to which I'd answer, "as often as you feel compelled to do so". As long as you remain interested in the role and feel as though there's a message to share that may have value or relate in some way to the content of your original conversations I say go for it always keeping in mind the adages of Mark Joyner noted earlier in this book...

1. What are you selling? 2. What will it cost me? 3. Why should I believe you? 4. What's in it for me?

Your follow-up is really important. Don't just slough it off and be real intangible about it.

Be the same person all the time.

Everything you do, every message you have, must look, feel, sound and take the form of *consistent authenticity*. The TRUTH really will set you and your career free. You just have to know what the TRUTH is, and use it on and on and on again, and people will start to pay attention.

Your **MESSAGE** will reek with authenticity.

There's certainly a chance people may not like it, but that's okay. You're not going to be liked by everybody. You just need to be liked and appreciated by the people who like you for your **MESSAGE**, for who you are, for what you're about.

As one of my teachers said, *"As soon as you try to be everything to everybody, you'll be nothing to anybody."*

In a nutshell, that's how you follow-up.

All that you've just read is "How The TRUTH Will Set You and Your Career Free".

I'm as sure as sure can be that if you've paid attention and don't eliminate any of the steps of the process, try not to use "magic trick" action to fix complex issues, you'll be more free and more sane than you could ever imagine

"How the TRUTH Will Set You & Your Career Free" - Not So Hidden TRUTH

I wanted this book to have 11 chapters so I could use the Spinal Tap/Nigel Tufnel quote above...even though there are 12 chapters, I used it anyway...I can tell Nigel if I see him that "our book goes to 12".

That's the TRUTH and I'm sticking to it...I challenge you to find, tell and use yours 24/7/365...the freedom will be astounding.

If you're interested in more information on any TRUTHS discussed in these pages, whether speaking, private consults, group training or "Do it with you" hands-on training to get your

"How the TRUTH Will Set You & Your Career Free" systems built please feel free to write to me.

truth@barrykleiman.com and write More Truth in the SUBJECT line

EPILOGUE

" When you come to a fork in the road...take it"

- Yogi Berra

Yogi Berra and The Critical Few

Pretty much all of these pages resolve to that famous quote from the iconic New York Yankee catcher...
(He had many...maybe someday I'll write a book about each, though choosing the one above seemed the perfect epilogue for this book)

At least as far as I can recall there have been very few days in my life during the past 40+ years that has not included being involved in a conversation or two with someone at the proverbial "fork in the road" in their own life, their own career or both.

One could argue that forks are ubiquitous...that each of us in one way or another is always coming to or presently standing right in front of one of those tined objects.

Every day...multiple times an hour "we" arrive at "forks" in some way, shape or form. Some more profound than others, but, from brushing one's teeth in the morning (or not) to whether to have that donut vs. the gluten-free waffle or the coffee vs tea etc etc...

"Forks" are everywhere and it's our decisions at those points that ultimately define us humanoids.

The goal of this entire collection of empirically based commentary is to ask you to consider:

The TRUTH...your TRUTHS, not mine!

What's Important Now (W.I.N), WHY it's important and ultimately to HOW to TAKE ACTION on those things!!

In his song **Growin' Up,** Bruce Springsteen sings *"I stood stonelike at midnight, suspended in my masquerade".*

I count myself as one of the many people who stood "stonelike" essentially suspended in my own masquerade...paralyzed by my own fear...happier to be unhappy than uncertain...ultimately playing out precious days in some sort of resigned resolved state of being.

"It's just the way it is", we tell ourselves...

We further rationalize this suspended animation with excuses that things were either:
1. Too hard or
2. Not exactly right, or
3. Worried about what others may say/think or
4. Worried about the consequences of losing something (that ironically was often the source of the misery in the first place).

FYI...I numbered the above list so as to evoke a mini-contest if you're up for it. How many excuses can you add to it? They could be your own or those of a friend, loved one, etc. Go ahead...give it a go. If you're being TRUTHFUL I bet you'll come up with more excuses than the paltry four I listed!

Anyway...if you've come to these pages I'm hoping it's not because you were seeking the next Hemingway...my writing style is obviously a long way from perfect.

My guess is you are reading this or other books of this genre because at some level you are now or rapidly approaching "a fork" and trying to figure out whether or not to proceed from being "suspended in your masquerade" then how best to proceed if that's your want.

I'm gonna go way far out on a limb here and say you want to move out of suspended animation but are seeking some trigger, methodology or paradigm shift to assist you.

Well, I've shared with you my views, mindsets, as well as some of the techniques and methodologies to navigate "forks"; it's really up to you now to take one of them! It's really up to you to toss away the "rather be unhappy than be uncertain" mindset and MOVE...trust yourself!

Do the work discussed in these pages or burn them and follow the dogma of another but get yourself out of suspended animation!!!!

The Pareto Principle: The Critical Few vs. The Trivial Many
I spoke often in these pages about the "1%" (critical few) and the fact that those people are dubbed as such because they clearly have separated themselves from the rest ("the trivial many").
*Back in the 1800's an Italian economist named Vilfredo Pareto shared with the world his 80/20 observation about the distribution of wealth in Italy...80% of the wealth was held by 20% of the people. His now well-known "Pareto Principle" has since been applied to many other areas of life, science and business telling us that the **critical few** are the minority of anything that contribute to the majority of the upside effects of that same thing.*

How The Truth Will Set You & Your Career Free

YOU WANT TO BE ONE OF THE **CRITICAL FEW** and there's really only one way...

Take a fork! That's what the critical few do!
Those who get stuff done take forks...well reasoned but action nonetheless (vs. being "suspended in your masquerade").

PICK A QUOTE....ANY QUOTE!

You miss 100% of the shots you don't take! – Wayne Gretzky

Action is the TRUE measure of intelligence - Napoleon Hill

Talk doesn't cook rice – Old Chinese Proverb

Well, TRUST YOURSELF, start with the TRUTH then...

TAKE A SHOT!

BE INTELLIGENT!

COOK SOME RICE!

Freedom begins just on the other side of whatever action you take!

If I can be of any further assistance please feel free to reach out.
truth@barrykleiman.com
In the SUBJECT line write: Fork in the Road

Yours TRULY,

Barry